LOVING ENEMIES

LOVING ENEMIES

A Manual for Ordinary People

Randy and Joyce Klassen

Foreword by
Robert K. Johnston

Publishing House
Telford, Pennsylvania

copublished with
Herald Press
Scottdale, Pennsylvania

Cascadia Publishing House LLC orders, information, reprint permissions:
contact@cascadiapublishinghouse.com
1-215-723-9125
126 Klingerman Road, Telford PA 18969
www.CascadiaPublishingHouse.com

Loving Enemies
Copyright © 2008 by Cascadia Publishing House
a division of Cascadia Publishing House LLC, Telford, PA 18969
All rights reserved.
Copublished with Herald Press, Scottdale, PA
Library of Congress Catalog Number: 2008034493
ISBN 13: 978-1-931038-53-9; **ISBN 10:** 1-931038-53-8
Book design by Cascadia Publishing House and cover design by
Merrill R. Miller based on drawing by Randy Klassen. Author photos
used by permission of Olan Mills.

The paper used in this publication is recycled and meets the
minimum requirements of American National Standard for Information Sciences—Permanence of Paper for Printed Library Materials,
ANSI Z39.48-1984.

All Bible quotations are used by permission, all rights reserved and,
unless otherwise noted, are from *The New Revised Standard Version of
the Bible*, copyright 1989, by the Division of Christian Education of the
National Council of the Churches of Christ in the USA.

Library of Congress Cataloguing-in-Publication Data
Klassen, Randolph J.
  Loving enemies : a manual for ordinary people / Randy and
Joyce Klassen ; foreword by Robert K. Johnston.
    p. cm.
  Includes bibliographical references.
  ISBN-13: 978-1-931038-53-9 (5.5 x 8.5" trade pbk. : alk. paper)
  ISBN-10: 1-931038-53-8 (5.5 x 8.5" trade pbk. : alk. paper)
 1. Love--Religious aspects--Christianity. 2. Peace--Religious aspects--Christianity. I. Klassen, Joyce, 1936- II. Title.

BV4639.K53 2008
241'.4--dc22

2008034493

15 13 12 11 10 09 08   10 9 8 7 6 5 4 3 2

*To all who long for peace
and act in ways that
help it happen*

Contents

Foreword: The Illogic of Grace, by Robert K. Johnston   8
Acknowledgements   11
Authors' Preface   13

1 We Are Not Impressed by the
   Record of World Religions • 21
2 We Are Disappointed by Our Culture of Violence • 32
3 We Are Moved by Jesus' Identification with Sinners • 41
4 We Are Impressed by How Jesus Faced His Enemies • 48
5 We Are Inspired by What Jesus Taught About Love • 54
6 We Are Challenged by How the Early Church Loved • 61
7 We Need to Learn How to End Prejudice • 67
8 We Are Sad That Countries Still
   Choose the Futility of War • 73
9 We Are Impressed by Nonviolent Success • 80
10 We Are Inspired by Stories of Nonviolence in Action • 90
11 We Are Healed by the Role of Forgiveness • 98
12 We Are Challenged by the Biblical
   Call to Justice and Peace • 108
13 We Ask, Could We Have Chosen a More
   Excellent Way After 9-11? • 114
14 We Are Convinced of the Supremacy
   of the Law of Love • 122
15 We Share Letters of Yearning for Peace • 132
   Conclusion • 142

Notes   143
The Authors   147

Foreword:
The Illogic of Grace

I CAN'T REMEMBER MOST SERMONS, even soon after hearing them. But I do recall almost verbatim one meditation given over thirty years ago by David Hubbard, then president of Fuller Seminary, on "The Most Surprising Word in Scripture."

Not a noun or a verb, not even an adjective or adverb, the word Hubbard proclaimed that day was the lowly conjunction *therefore*! His text was the second chapter of Hosea, where the word is used three times. *Therefore* links cause with effect, antecedent with what follows. It recognizes the logic of life. Stay out in the sun, therefore you'll burn. Eat two pieces of chocolate pie, therefore you'll feel bloated.

Such logic is found in the book of Hosea as well. Called by God to marry the prostitute Gomer, Hosea discovers that the mother of his children has remained promiscuous. She has gone after lovers who would lavish on her oil and wine, wool and linen. In this regard, she is like the nation Israel, a living parable. Living a life of economic luxury, Israel too was in the midst of an "adulterous affair," adding to her worship of Yahweh her worship of Baal, the God of the harvest.

And so in chapter two, Hosea speaks God's word of judgment with two strong, preliminary "therefores." Gomer (Israel) has been unfaithful; *therefore*, Hosea, like God, will hedge up his beloved (v. 6). She is promiscuous; *therefore*, he will strip her naked and destroy her vineyards (v. 9). Violence is deserved; therefore it is declared.

But it was not these first two "therefores" that David Hubbard preached on that day. In Hosea, judgment and violence are announced but superseded by God's loving embrace. After Gomer's sin (after Israel's sin and our sin), God speaks through his prophet Hosea a third, surprising, and transforming "therefore." It is not based on our actions; it lacks any antecedent. Instead, this "therefore" comes solely from the character of God. Speaking through the prophet Hosea, God says,

> *Therefore*, I will now allure her. . . .
> . . . I will give her her vineyards. . . .
> . . . I will remove the names of the Baals from her mouth. . . .
> I will take you for my wife in faithfulness. . . . (2:14-20)

Here is a "therefore" that defies all human logic, one rooted solely in God himself. I can hear Hubbard's words ring out: "To the logical word of judgment, Hosea adds the illogical word of God's grace."

Rather than have Gomer stoned (something according to the law of the day that was within his rights), Hosea is to woo Gomer back by the strength of his continuing love. He is to create in her a new affection by his relentless, extravagant, illogical love.

As I read Randy and Joyce's book, I am reminded of God's (il)logical command to Hosea. In a post-9-11 world, is it not our right to hem in terrorism and destroy it? Such "therefores" make all the sense in the world. But just as Hosea's contagious love shows us a better way, so the Klassens remind us how inspired we become by the illogic of nonviolence, how moved we are by the redemptive role of forgiveness, how alluring and inviting are examples like those of Martin Luther King or Christians in the Philippines.

Hosea's name is a variant of "Joshua," from which we get the name "Jesus." What God revealed to Hosea, he fully incarnated in Jesus: "Love your enemies." "Turn the other cheek." Forgive as you would be forgiven."

Last week, while driving home from Santa Barbara, I smiled at the bumper sticker on the car ahead: "MAKE CUPCAKES, NOT WAR." It was from a bakery in town.

"Absurd," you say. Yes, but no more so than God's command to Hosea to woo Gomer back. "Illogical," you say. Surely, but so too, thankfully, is the love of God. Now, just as in Hosea's day, it is not the logical word of judgment that is needed but the surprising word of God's grace.

I invite you to read the prophetic, yet humble words of the Klassens—two "Christ-ones," two Christians, who would have each of us imitate Jesus/Joshua/Hosea.

—*Robert K. Johnston*
Fuller Theological Seminary

Acknowledgments

WE WISH TO EXPRESS OUR SINCERE INDEBTEDNESS to family members and friends who graciously took the time to read over our first drafts and offer constructive criticisms. Their contributions have improved this book.

We are grateful for the insights of Randy's sons, Timothy and Stephen who, being as deeply committed to nonviolence as we are, offered excellent thoughts on and illustrations of forgiveness and reconciliation.

Our special friends, Jonathan and Melissa Webster, gave very helpful advice, especially in the area of historical accuracy, where Jonathan's scholarship shines.

Rev. James Hawkinson, the former executive secretary of Covenant Publications and editor of the *Covenant Companion*, as well as a personal friend, also added excellent insights.

Randy's cousins, Herb and Maureen Klassen, both scholars and presently working with Logos International, offered their perceptive comments.

Michael A. King, Mennonite pastor; editor, *Dreamseeker Magazine*; and publisher, Cascadia Publishing House LLC, has guided Randy with his two previous publications: *Jesus' Word, Jesus' Way* (Herald Press), and *What Does the Bible Really Say About Hell?* (Pandora Press U.S., now a division of Cascadia LLC). He again offered sound direction for this manuscript.

Joyce's son, Jeff, an English major and journalist, did a critical review of the language and grammar. His wife,

Melissa, faithfully typed out the first draft of the manuscript, a job made more difficult since most of Randy's work was done in his sometimes not too legible longhand style.

Thanks also to Wayne Zeitner, a friend and critic who helped us maintain a balanced approach to an admittedly controversial subject.

In appreciation for their work on behalf of loving enemies, all profits from the sales of this book will be donated to the world relief ministries of the Mennonite Central Committee (MCC), the Evangelical Covenant Church, and the United Methodist Committee on Relief (UMCOR).

We are most grateful to these dear people who took their time to help us get across the message of "love in action" in the best literary form of which we are capable. Many thanks to each.

—*Randy and Joyce Klassen*
Walla Walla, Washington

Authors' Preface

RETURNING FROM PARTICIPATING IN AN ART SHOW in the Bay area, I stopped for a coffee break in Sacramento. It was late, and I did not see him. But just a few feet from my parked car, someone struck my head from behind, then my face. My glasses were broken and my money taken. I was left bloodied and dazed. The mugger disappeared. Forgiveness was not the first thought that came to mind.

My wife Joyce experienced the tragedy of an abusive childhood. Her mother assaulted her both verbally and physically, telling Joyce she wished she had never been born. The scars of that kind of abuse last a lifetime. Forgiveness was not Joyce's first reaction.

Her dad was in the U.S. Navy during World War II. While he was on his aircraft carrier, a Japanese kamikaze pilot struck, killing and injuring many. Her dad was among the injured. As we think of those killed or severely injured by the enemy in that or any war, we admit that forgiveness is not foremost in our hearts.

So whether the "enemy" is a personal assailant, a family member, or another nation, the biblical command to "love our enemies" sounds so unrealistic we tend to dodge it. This is a command for saints, not ordinary people. We proceed to a more enjoyable passage, like the one about God providing "wine to gladden the human heart" (Ps. 104:15). But even after that glass of wine, the troubling question of how to love our enemies remains. Since it was Jesus who said it, how can we claim allegiance to him if we ignore his command?

So this book is first of all written for us, two struggling Christians, ordinary people and not saints, seeking to understand the meaning and application of this radical teaching of Jesus. We write not as experts but simply as Christians longing to deepen our understanding and practical grasp of Jesus' Way of love. As our use of sources suggests, we borrow often from others and make no claim to original scholarship. If we have anything original to offer, we hope it grows, precisely, from our daily walk, imperfect as it is.

We are also writing to add our support and encouragement to those who not only long for peace but are thoughtfully and actively involved in doing what they can to advance justice and love for God's children everywhere. We are not referring to the fanatical fringe whose protests incite more violence than peace. We have in mind persons like Jim Wallis, President Jimmy Carter, Bishop Tutu, members of the Fellowship of Reconciliation (FOR), Mother Teresa, and the thousands who care enough to act on their convictions.

This will include the peace churches like the Brethren, Mennonite, Quaker, and other groups. They may well have read or heard much of what is included in this book. However, we hope that by hearing some of the old stories in a fresh context and by hearing some exciting new ones, such readers will feel strengthened and supported in their courageous resolve to "wage peace" in our troubled world.

The third group we feel strongly about addressing is made up of our fellow Christians in all churches. We claim the Bible as our guide. We share a commitment to Jesus and his teaching. We know he has called us to love our enemy, but this is so difficult we have often sidestepped the teaching or reinterpreted it to mean something safer or easier. So we pray that the thoughts and illustrations which arose during our journey and are now in this book will enable our brothers and sisters to reconsider, if necessary, understandings of this difficult command of Christ. We pray that you might then consider turning such insight into action.

A fourth group in our target audience includes anyone, regardless of religious affiliation or none, who longs for justice and peace. We hope you will find inspiration and reassurance from the stories and affirmations in the following chapters.

Above all, however, we simply hope to be helpful to ordinary people. Particularly since the time of Constantine, Christians have been tempted to see loving enemies as the calling of an occasional saint or saintly group. But what if Jesus intends this teaching for every Christian? Then we need a manual for how live this out in our ordinary lives. We hope this book provides at least the beginnings of such a manual.

At this point let me share a brief personal introduction. Though now a naturalized citizen of the United States, I (Randy), was born into a Mennonite Brethren family in Winnipeg, Canada. As a kid I did not like our church. All its participants spoke German, and in the 1940s we were at war with Germany. I also disliked the legalism of the church forbidding movies and dances which, as a high school student, I wanted to enjoy. When my dad donned a uniform of the navy reserve, I was proud of him. He never touched a gun, but as a patriotic Canadian he felt he was doing his part while keeping his pacifist commitment. The church, however, was not happy to see him in uniform, so we left for a more mainline church.

I came to make a commitment to Christ primarily through the witness of the InterVarsity Christian Fellowship. Their motto: "To Know Christ and To Make Him Known." I liked that. It was simple and to the point.

Feeling a call to ministry, I was directed by our InterVarsity staff person to attend Fuller Theological Seminary in Pasadena, California. It was a great experience for me until my funds ran out and I returned to Winnipeg. While there I was surprised by a call to serve as interim pastor of Teien Covenant Church, just south of the border, in Minnesota. When I asked what the doctrinal position of the Covenant denomination was, I was told: "You preach Christ, and we will pray for you"

"Is that it?" I asked in amazement.

The pulpit committee chairperson, Adolph Anderson, responded, "Is there more?" I joined the Covenant church that moment.

For the next forty years I served in the Covenant denomination doing mostly pastoral ministry, with some teaching, writing, administration, and new church development. I appreciated the inclusiveness of the Covenant denomination combined with keeping the focus on Jesus Christ and biblical authority. What the Bible has to say on any subject is important to me.

As the global climate seems increasingly disrupted by storms of war and violence in our own land rises, thoughts of how to bring about peace in our world have come increasingly to the forefront of my thinking. I had once rejected the Mennonite position of nonresistance, but now I am taking another look at what it really meant. After all, it was Jesus who said, "Love your enemies." If I am to be a follower of Jesus, I must take seriously what he commanded. What could he possibly have meant? Maybe my Mennonite ancestors grasped something I had missed.

So, now in retirement, I am giving this subject a more careful study. Besides the Bible, I am reading authors like John Howard Yoder, Walter Wink, Ronald Sider, Jim Wallis, Richard Hayes, Marcus Borg, Pitirim Sorokin, and others who take seriously Jesus' command to love enemies.

As I shared such thoughts with my wife Joyce, she became increasingly involved in developing the manuscript. Through perceptive critiques, comments, and suggestions, her passion for peacemaking led her to co-author this book. Forgiveness plays an essential role in peacemaking. And forgiveness has been an especially significant aspect of Joyce's experience. She shares her insights in chapter eleven. Later, as we continued to draft the manuscript, Joyce was challenged by one critic to deal with the United States reaction to September 11, 2001. The result became chapter thirteen.

To most of us, the idea of showing love to an enemy sounds like a totally impossible, impractical, unrealistic, and unattainable ethic. Doesn't world history show it doesn't work? Human wisdom decrees that bad people and bad nations must not be allowed to continue in their evil ways. Popular culture believes we need to rid our world of the "bad guys." So we sanction state enforcement of the death penalty for murderers and for "noble" reasons justify going to war. After all, if these countries are a part of the "axis of evil," they must be punished for their wickedness. We cannot allow them to threaten us or allies. We cannot allow criminals to get away with destructive behavior. Is it not reasonable that some may have to die to make this a better world? Are we not virtuous for daring to be their executioners? This, at least, has been common thinking and practice for centuries.

In *The Powers That Be*, Walter Wink calls such a response the "myth of redemptive violence" and says that "It enshrines the belief that violence saves, that war brings peace, that might makes right. It is one of the oldest repeated stories in the world."[1] This belief doesn't seem mythic because it appears to be both inevitable and practical. It is an ancient creed that seems to be present in every society in every age, even though its practice has never won a lasting peace. However, here and there another method has been practiced. The results surprised us and may surprise you as well.

This other method was not given a strong emphasis in the two fine seminaries I attended. I cannot recall significant references to Jesus' teaching about enemy love. These schools honored biblical authority, but "how to overcome evil with good" was not a required course. The witness of the church was couched more in personal terms than as an embodiment of God's justice, love, and peace in this world. Thankfully, this has changed to a significant degree, and probably will even more in the days ahead. Hopefully, this will include more and more Christian seminaries and churches.

In the following chapters we hope you will see that "enemy love" may not be as unrealistic or even as impractical as it sounds. Jesus called on his followers to "love your enemies" (Matt. 5:44), and he lived out that teaching. Other sages have also recognized that killing humans is wrong, but often exceptions are cited, as indeed they have been in most Christian denominations. But a careful reading of the text reveals that Jesus allowed for no exceptions. We will consider his ethic of a nonviolent resistance to evil as a positive not a negative action. We will note that it takes courage, commitment, creativity, and sacrifice to overcome evil with good—and it *is* possible.

The prayer of Saint Francis of Assisi has inspired millions, and it is also our prayer for this book.

> O Lord, make me an instrument of your peace.
> Where there is hatred, let me sow love.
> Where there is injury, pardon.
> Where there is doubt, faith.
> Where there is despair, hope.
> Where there is darkness, light.
> Where there is sadness, joy.
> O Divine Master,
> Let me not so much seek
> to be consoled, as to console,
> to be understood, as to understand,
> to be loved, as to love.
> For it is in giving that we receive,
> It is in pardoning that we are pardoned
> It is in dying that we are born to eternal life. Amen

In some small way, we pray that this book's engagement with loving the enemy will be for any of us, however ordinary, however sinful as well as saintly, an instrument of God's peace. May any insights gleaned in our efforts to prepare and offer this manual strengthen our mutual resolve to become actively involved in being the "peacemakers" Jesus called "blessed." This is the challenge: to embrace a selfless and positive love for our enemies, a love that wills the best for those who seem to will the worst for us.

LOVING ENEMIES

Chapter One

We Are Not Impressed by the Record of World Religions

*H*ERE IS A FRIGHTENING COMMENT. The history of the world is a history of warfare with intervals of peace. Gavin D. Becker states that "violence is a part of our species. It is around us and it is in us . . . a force of nature, a permanent and regular feature of mankind."[2] If that is the case, shouldn't it be religion that makes things better?

Religion addresses the motives of the heart, so one would think that religions would play a decisive role in bringing peace into our world. Most religions do advocate kindness and love for neighbor and condemn cruelty and murder. But is that what we see?

It doesn't seem so. When we take a closer look at our violent history, we discover how often religion plays a role in justifying the killing of enemies. Religion becomes a useful tool to encourage the conviction that "I'm right—so you're wrong." "If God is on our side, he's not on yours." It is then but a short step from condemnation to supposedly deserved punishment.

The Christian community rarely played that role until it was embraced by Rome in 313 CE, under Emperor Constantine. Suddenly the persecuting empire became the "professing church" in one of the most dramatic about-faces in history. It became an empire in which what the emperor willed, the church supported; and what the church leaders willed, the emperor supported—with the sword. By 385 CE, under the rule of Theodosius, the empire was persecuting non-Christians. In the ninth century it became officially known as "The 'Holy' Roman Empire." The wedding of church and state had been achieved. And the idea of love for the enemy was lost.

There were, of course, sensitive souls who did challenge the ways of the emperor. Augustine in the fourth century decried the meaningless bloodshed of groundless battles and so began to expound a "just war" theory. Over the centuries since, this theory has been reworked many times in an effort to provide a series of criteria by which war might be considered permissible. If these requirements are met, then war is justifiable. Although it would involve killing, Augustine felt that the intentions of the combatants mattered more than attempting to take literally the biblical part about loving the enemy.

So theologians over the years have debated about what constitutes a "just war" and how it can harmonize with the teachings of Jesus. Is there a clear offense or injury that needs to be redressed? Has every diplomatic attempt been made to solve the dispute? Can the damage of a proposed war be less than the damage inflicted? Will it be waged along moral lines? Will it be declared by a proper authority? Has everything been tried? Will it be a last resort? The fact that Jesus rejected all forms of violence as a legitimate treatment of enemies is set aside. Other Scriptures are found and used.

While both the Qur'an and the New Testament rule out any "pre-emptive strike" (the Rodwell translation of The Koran in Sura 2 reads, "commit not the injustice of attacking them first," and Jesus call to love our enemies),we do find in nearly all the religious source books support for killing an enemy. These references are usually phrased as exceptions to the law, "you shall not kill," which, by the way, is also included in the scriptures of most religions. These can be can be seen when checking the index of *World Scripture: A Com-*

parative Anthology of Sacred Texts (a project of the International Religious Foundation published by Paragon House in 1995).

Some Biblical scholars have noted that in the Hebrew Bible there are six hundred passages of explicit violence, a thousand verses describing God's violent punishments, and about a hundred passages in which Yahweh commands the killing of others. After learning this, I checked several references and found that Moses believed God was commanding him to take revenge on the Midianites for what they had done to the Israelites. He was to "kill every adult male . . . and every male among the little ones and every married woman" (Num. 31:7, 17). Again, in a call against foreign towns, the command was to "let not anything that breathes remain alive. You shall annihilate them" (Deut. 20:16). Is this the biblical teaching about loving the enemy?

Killing was not only for enemy peoples or nations. Within Israel death was a legal punishment not only for murder but also for rebellious sons (Deut. 21:18); adulterers (Lev. 20:10-11); homosexuals (Lev. 20:13); fortunetellers or mediums (Lev. 21:27); those who curse God (Lev. 24:15); or those who work on the Sabbath (Exod. 31:14-15).

Joyce and I had some early exposure to those Christians who claim to take the Bible literally. Passages like the above didn't seem to upset them; or maybe they didn't notice them. They disturbed us. They did not sound like the God whom Jesus revealed, the God he called "Abba," Father. But if we do take those passages literally, they provide an easy justification for killing.

As artists, we take an understandable interest in the works of other artists. So we were delighted to receive a copy of the famous edition of the *The Doré Bible Illustrations* reproducing the 1800s artwork of Gustav Doré. We soon noticed that almost half of the 241 plates pictured in the 1974 edition released by Dover Publications picture subjects of violence. A "picture is worth a thousand words." Is that really what the Bible is about?

Admittedly, the Old Testament does contain over a hundred verses about fighting and killing the enemy. Our book has to do with what the Bible says about loving the enemy, and there is little about that until we come upon a verse like this one, in Proverbs 16:7, "When the ways of the people please the Lord, he causes even their enemies to live at peace with them." Here is another verse that reminds us of what Jesus said, "If your enemies are hungry, give them bread to eat; and if they are thirsty, give them water to drink" (Prov. 25:21). The prophet Isaiah looked for a day when "the boots of trampling warriors shall be burned" and the coming Messiah would be a "Prince of Peace" (Isa. 9:5-6). They "will beat their swords into plowshares" and "neither shall they learn war any more" (Isa. 2:4). The early church wondered if this would be fulfilled as they sought to participate in the kingdom of God by their allegiance to Jesus.

Until 313 CE, the church was committed to nonviolence. But after Constantine embraced Christianity, the church became almost indistinguishable from its surrounding culture and so became a part of a political movement that justified aggression against all enemies. It is understandable that by using the Hebrew Scriptures the church could find justification for killing the enemy. The way of Jesus was set aside .By 385 CE all non-Christians in the Roman Empire and in conquered territories were considered enemies and as such punishable by death if they failed to convert. Talk about high-pressure evangelism!

This deadly approach continued into the Middle Ages, when the Crusades claimed the lives of tens of thousands of Muslims, Jews, and other "nonbelievers." While the motivation was usually a mix of religious, political, or economic factors, the justification was nearly always couched in religious terms such as to free the Holy Land from the Unbelievers. To claim God as being on their side validated any actions they took, regardless of the extent of cruelty or loss of life. Painting the cross on the Crusaders' shields declared their Christian allegiance, although most of the participants knew nothing about the teachings of Jesus. Adding a verse from the Bible about killing the wicked was all it took to bolster their zeal.

Sadly, this attitude still prevails. While preparing this manuscript we read a letter to the editor in our local paper in which a writer said that she thought "Jesus would be *pleased*" that as Americans we had chosen to take out the Iraqi dictator, Saddam Hussein. That the cost of this war included over tens of thousands of fatalities, mostly innocent civilians, including women and children, was not acknowledged in her letter. We do not recognize *that* Jesus in the New Testament. Our feeling is that Jesus would *weep* at such action. In fact, he did, as he entered Jerusalem, lamenting, "If you, even you, had only known the things that make for peace" (Luke 19:42). They were blind then as we appear to be today.

Church-sponsored violence continued through the twelfth century, when the popes launched crusades against those whom they considered heretics. Groups like the Cathars, the Waldensians, and the Albigensians were indeed cultic in some ways that diverted from orthodox doctrine, but their condemnation of the established church was especially irritating to the pope and church leaders. Their growth posed a threat to the church, especially in southern France, so they had to be stopped. Even torture was condoned to secure repentance. If this failed, burning at the stake was the ultimate punishment.

Another justification for the violence sanctioned by the church was its theology of a literal hell. Randy's son Stephen in conversation with his dad put it like this:

> Historically that idea of hell has been a primary justification for torture, war, and other violence. There is logic in this. If God uses extreme violence, then couldn't he use his servants to do this work? During the Inquisition, the church considered their tortures merciful compared to hell. First of all, what could a mere human do that would equal the eternal agonies of hell? Second, if by torture one could convince the accused to confess their heresy, then we would have saved them from the infinitely worse punishment of hell.

After the Reformation in the sixteenth century, there seemed to be a renewed interest in biblical teaching. Luther's translation of the Bible into the German language, and Guttenburg's printing press, were making the Bible more available. Yet even with their increased knowledge of the New Testament, both Luther and Calvin allowed for violence against the heretics who challenged their interpretations. Sadly, Luther even encouraged violence against all "heretics" or "revolutionaries" as evidenced in the bloody Peasants War of 1525. The major clashes, however, between Catholics and Protestants continued until the terrible "Thirty Years War" (1618–1648). Minor clashes have continued and in parts of Northern Ireland violence has only faded (we hope) at the beginning of the twenty-first century.

Islam has experienced a similar history. Mohammed was faced with warring factions from the beginning. When Islam achieved a period of peace, it was interrupted by the Crusades in the Middle Ages and in the eighteenth and nineteenth centuries by Western colonialism. Some Muslim scholars have claimed that by 1918 there was not a Muslim in the world who did not live in a country under foreign subjugation. As some of these lands became more independent, clashes between Islamic sects would break out, claiming a large death toll. In the war between Iraq and Iran, over a million were killed.

Although the Qur'an states that there is to be "no compulsion in religion," Christian, Jewish, and Hindu groups have suffered Muslim violence in various parts of our world. Muslim extremists, or fundamentalists, as some are called, continue acts of violence, choosing the verses from the Qur'an that fit their agendas, as other religious groups have done. Its Scriptures contain many "war verses." The prophet Mohammed urged his followers to "fight those of the unbelievers who are near you and let them find in you hardness" (9:123, MK Shakir ed.). "Those who reject Islam must be killed. If they turn back (from Islam) take them and kill them wherever you find them" (4:89, the Noble Qur'an ed.) . "O you who believe! Retaliation is prescribed for you in the matter of the slain . . . there is life for you in [the law of] retaliation" (2:178, 179). The "eye for an eye" mandate in the Hebrew Bible, intended as a limiting measure for justice, has become an incentive for vengeance.

In a 2006 PBS interview with an imam near his mosque in England, the Islamic leader stated that it was the sacred duty of all Muslims to wage a "jihad," or holy war, against unbelievers. These "infidels" are going against the will of God, and therefore must be attacked. If they repent and turn to Islam, they will be spared, but a heathen nation like the Unites States, with all of its greed, pornography, and drunkenness, must be destroyed. He went on to say that faithful Muslims accept every letter of every word in the Qur'an as binding. Therefore verses like the following must be obeyed:

"You will fight against them until they submit" (66:9).

"Fight against them until there is no more *Fitnah* [disbelief] and the religion will all be for Allah alone" (8:39 The Noble Qur'an).

"O prophet, urge the believers to war" (8:65).

This imam would be considered a fundamentalist, as is Osama bin Laden, a greatly admired hero among many Muslims. Some of his admirers who grew up in England decided that the British too were infidels deserving death. So in summer 2005 they launched several suicide bomb attacks in the subways and buses of London, killing and wounding many. More moderate or liberal Muslims consider such actions a disgrace. Some of them have participated in nonviolent peace groups like Fellowship of Reconciliation (FOR) and have established the Muslim Peace Fellowship. Read what Hossein Alizadeh has to say at www.MPFweb.org. He is a bold spokesperson for justice and peace.

A personal friend of ours is a Sufi Muslim. A kinder and more generous man would be hard to find. He helped Hope Covenant Church, which I was serving as developer pastor, find a suitable place to worship in the strip mall that he managed in Chandler, Arizona. He made the rent affordable and went to bat for us when some other renters expressed concerns about a church moving in. He helped us understand that the Sufi sect is the more mystical and peace-loving branch of the Muslim faith, while the Wahhabis are more rigid and prone to violence in advancing their cause.

Hebrew, Muslim, Buddhist, and Hindu Scriptures contain beautiful verses about mercy and peace. We will share some of these in our last chapter. The dream of most is beautifully expressed in these words from the Hebrew Bible: God "shall arbitrate for many peoples; they shall beat their swords into plowshares' and their spears into pruning hooks; nation shall not lift up sword against nation, neither shall they learn war any more" (Isa. 2:4).

However, when an enemy appears, the "war verses" are chosen. The concept of "neighbor love," found in most religions, is nearly always modified by statements regarding exceptions. Murder is condemned, but in the case of law-breaking, self defense, preventing greater crimes, violating a political border, or threatening national security, then the "just cause" is invoked to sanction killing the enemy.

Buddhist and Hindu Scriptures also contain messages of love and peace. Yet here also the enemies of Dharma, Buddhist truth, or Hindu moral law can be subject to death for their defiance. Much of the bloodshed in India in the mid-twentieth century, despite Gandhi's courageous intervention, happened in battles between Hindus and Muslims. This finally resulted in the partition of the land, creating the country of Pakistan and later Bangladesh.

Violence has been a part of the fabric of American culture from the beginning. Much of it was motivated by religious convictions. The Puritans, who came to the New World because of persecution in their homeland, soon proceeded to persecute their new neighbors who failed to conform to Puritan ways. To build a "Christian empire," they took action against the heathen (Native Americans), the heretics (Catholics and Quakers), so-called witches, and others who failed their litmus test.

When African slaves were brought to our shores, centuries of cruelty began, supported by preachers using Bible texts to justify the institution of slavery. When emancipation finally came in 1865, the situation for our black neighbors did not immediately improve. Between 1870 and 1940, over 5,000 lynchings of blacks were recorded; most of these supported by the corrupt religion of the Ku Klux Klan. Blatant racism is less common in America today, but systemic and more subtle forms continue to be expressed.

Religious extremists insist upon conformity to their understanding of what is right. When some in their region fail to conform, violence is unleashed. Protestants against Catholics in New England, one polygamous Mormon cult against another in Utah, Hasidic against Sephardic Jews in New York, and the list could go on to cover pages.

Thankfully, much of the religiously inspired violence in our country has ended. Protestants, Catholics, Jews, and other major religious communities are living in peace with one another. Many are even working together to advance the causes of tolerance and justice for all. However, some hate groups still exist and in a few areas are growing as they spread their message on the Internet.

There are some white supremacist groups who call themselves "Christian" that are avowedly anti-black and anti-Semitic. Their claim to be Christian is ludicrous, since Jesus Christ was Semitic (Jewish) and welcomed all races in his land. But it is true that ignorance is a strong ingredient in those violently intolerant of other perspectives.

Considering these and other cases in history, outspoken atheists like one-time leader of the American Atheist Society, Madelyn O'Hare, or more recently Sam Harris or Richard Dawkins in bestselling atheist manifestos, have claimed that religion is responsible for more deaths by warfare and inquisitions than any other cause. They are partly correct. But if our definition of religion includes a belief in God, then the Communist killing of millions in the Soviet Union can hardly be blamed on religion. Some might call Communism a religion, but its atheist dogmas would rule that out if we include God in our definition of religion. However, if religion is simply understood to be a "belief system," then those who give themselves to doctrines like the "Communist Manifesto" do manifest a type of religious zeal.

The bloodshed in Israel, Palestine, and Iraq in recent decades has brought to the headlines the religious zeal of suicide bombers who are willing to die if only they can take some "infidels" with them. For us in the United States, the never-to-be-forgotten tragedies of 9-11 are a clear reminder of what religious fanaticism can produce. Muslim extremists or fundamentalists find support in some of their mosques from a few imams who choose certain parts of the Qur'an to justify their acts of violence. The parts which condemn acts of violence against the innocent are ignored.

The American invasion of Iraq has reminded the Muslim world of the Christian Crusades of past centuries. The United States of America, claiming to be a Christian nation, has struck a Muslim nation. To many it seems that a religious war is once again being fought. By some estimates, hundreds of thousands have died and many more have been critically wounded. More will die because each side claims a moral justification for its warring ways.

Ever since Cain killed Abel, this planet has been drenched in the blood of fratricide, for each person we kill is a brother or a sister. Can we really make exceptions to the law of love?

While in a bookstore, I picked up a book by Leo Tolstoy I had not heard of before. In it, this wealthy count and successful author confessed to feeling empty and frustrated by what he saw in himself and in his world of the late nineteenth century. He started reading Scriptures from various religions and was profoundly impressed by the teachings of Jesus as recorded by Matthew in what has traditionally been called the "Sermon on the Mount." In this Scripture he discovered the "law of love" as the one and only way to personal, local, and world peace. Tolstoy saw the incarnation of divine love in Jesus. It was life-changing for him as he wrote in "A Confession" in 1882:

> Only by fulfilling the law of love in its true, rather limited meaning, i.e. as the supreme law that does not admit any exceptions, can we find salvation from the terrible, increasingly disastrous and apparently hopeless situation

of the "Christian" nations today. For a Christian who has recognized the demands of the law of love, none of the demands of the law of violence can be obligatory, but present themselves as human errors which must be exposed and abolished.[3]

Tolstoy is not a theologian, but how could it be better stated? He affirms a total commitment to the law of love, one that seems foreign to the thoughts and policies of many of our people and leaders today. They believe there are situations that legitimately call for a violent response. So they call on our religious leaders to support their causes of aggression. Sadly, many do.

But what does the Bible really say about killing the enemy? As Christians we believe God's Word comes to us most clearly in Jesus, whom the gospel writer, John, calls "the Word of God." And Jesus exhorts us to put down the sword and learn the discipleship art of loving the enemy.

We should have recognized that the record of religion would not all be positive. After all, wasn't it the religious establishment that insisted on the crucifixion of Jesus? There religion was the enemy, not the peacemaker.

In the next chapter, we shall consider other factors in our society which are conducive to violence. It appears that violence is ingrained in our culture.

Chapter Two

We Are Disappointed by Our Culture of Violence

*T*HE BIBLE REPORTS THAT HUMAN VIOLENCE goes back to earliest times. Genesis 6:11 reports that "the earth was filled with violence." Ezekiel laments that "the land ([srael] is full of bloody crimes; the city [Jerusalem] is full of violence" (Ezek. 7:23). God's people were expected to do better, but failure fills the histories of all people. Do we share an infection called "sin"? Some of those who first came to America aspired to do better. They cited lofty ideals and labeled their new land a "Christian nation." But look where we are today.

H. "Rap" Brown alleged in the 1960s (a decade drenched in violence) that "violence is as American as cherry pie." As noted in the previous chapter, bloodshed and mayhem are an integral part of our history from the arrival of our first explorers until this day. In attempting to understand why America is more violent than any of its peer nations, historians have pointed to the American Revolution as our birthing event, the Civil War as our unity preserving event, and the six-shooter as the way the West was won. If these violent actions supposedly produced a good result, then such actions must be justifiable, despite the damage incurred. So we have become accustomed to violence as something inevitable and even at times appropriate.

Although the past century saw an increase in violent crimes, it was back in 1837 that Abraham Lincoln declared "the mortal threat to American democracy is not a foreign military power, but an internal flaw: violence." Ronald Gottesman is editor-in-chief of a three-volume encyclopedia, *Violence in America*, published in 1999. In it he notes the broadly varied ways violence is represented in our culture. He writes, "Our dance, music, painting, sculpture, and literature as well as our comics, print and broadcast media, movies, television programming, folklore, sports, and even our everyday language, all bear witness to American practices of violence."[4]

The other day I went into a video store, not to rent a movie this time but to take a closer look at all the titles. Those identified under the captions of "comedy" or "musicals" had few hints of violence. Under "drama" there were many, but under "action" it seemed that ninety percent contained violence. When I checked the video games, the percentage containing violence seemed ninety percent or higher. These are the videos our kids are watching or playing. One game enables the player to participate in the assassination of President Kennedy. Another, for a so-called more "mature" audience, enables the player to sexually abuse a curvaceous enemy before beheading her!

The best-selling video game in the United States in 2004 was *Grand Theft Auto: San Andreas*. It sold 5.2 million copies. The National Institute on Media and the Family described its contents as "Raunchy, violent, and portraying just about every deviant act that a criminal could think of in full, living 3D graphics." Furthermore, "*Grand Theft Auto* takes the cake again as one of the years worst games for kids," wrote Mona Charen, a syndicated columnist.

The premise of this video is to restore respect to your neighborhood gang as you take on the corrupt San Andreas police. Game play features buying and selling drugs, stealing cars, foul language, racial slurs, running down pedestrians, attacking people with chainsaws, sexual jokes and in some versions sexual activity, killing police, and feeding people into a wood chopper. When young people consume such poison, how can we expect anything other than a sick result?

On a personal note, we were not only disgusted by hearing about this video game but offended by its name, since we lived in a quiet foothill town called San Andreas in California. It had a low crime rate and there was little evidence to suggest that our police were corrupt. Besides, San Andreas is Spanish for Saint Andrew, a wonderful man of God, hardly fitting as a name for such a godless video.

The profit motive, no doubt, determines much of what is produced in films, video games, and TV programs. Show the "bad" people in all their wickedness. Make it exciting by letting them win until almost the end, when our hero comes through to kill the evil ones. This fits with what Walter Wink labeled as the "myth of redemptive violence," which

> is the simplest, laziest, most exciting, uncomplicated, irrational, and primitive depiction of evil the world has ever known. Furthermore, its orientation toward evil is one into which virtually all modern children (boys especially) are socialized in the process of maturation.[5]

Thus, violence is made pleasurable and entertaining. So from earliest years, kids are seduced into believing that violence is the best solution to human conflict. I remember, as a kid, begging my dad for a toy gun. All the other kids had them, and it was such fun to play with them and kill all the bad guys.

Dad finally gave in—but got me a water pistol, not a cap gun.

Of course, not all movies are bad. Some films are beautiful, breathtaking, and challenging. Some are even redemptive, as Robert K. Johnston has pointed out in his perceptive study of theology and film in dialogue, *Reel Spirituality*, first published in 2000. Here he also supports some of the charges critics like Michael Medved have leveled against Hollywood, saying that "movies promote promiscuity, malign marriage, encourage illegitimacy, and belittle parents. They ... use foul language, often offend, and gravitate toward violence."[6] Some push violence to extreme limits, as in *Texas Chainsaw Massacre, The Evil Dead, Zombie Flesh Eaters,* or *Grand Theft*

Auto: San Andreas. In the most brutal films, violence becomes an end in itself. The violence is not so much intended to do in the bad guys as to create an addictive high, a pathetic aphrodisiac. What happens to the heart or soul of a person who finds enjoyment in cruelty and violence?

The human readiness to kill an enemy goes back to the beginning of history. I remember in history classes reading about the Pharaohs and the Caesars, the Goths and the Visigoths, the Mongols and the Vikings, and all of their bloody adventures. Those were cruel times, we were told. What I did not learn until the turn of the twenty-first century is that the twentieth century saw more deaths caused by warfare than in all of the wars in all of the preceding centuries! The overly optimistic liberal adage of the 1920s, "In every way, in every day, the world is getting better and better," has been proved false. The world is becoming more violent, not less. This is of course due in part to our use of weapons of mass destruction. We kill incredibly more with our bombs than was possible with a club or spear.

Our country was founded on ideals of freedom for all. Our history books praise the founding fathers for their courage and faith, and much of the praise is deserved. Heroism is not the full story, however. Our treatment of the native Americans, and later the importing and dehumanizing of African slaves, is a disgrace to a country that boasts of "justice and liberty for all."

Violence marks much of the story in settling America. I don't intend a review of U.S. history here except to indicate that the six-shooter was often the determiner of law and order. When we lived in the area of the 1849 Gold Rush, we heard many accounts of the violence of the greedy. Gold was the lure, and anyone in the way was expendable. Back in 1885, the town of Bodie, California, boasted a population of 10,000 people and "a murder a day."

Western movies, drawing on both history and legend, make heroes of the gunfighters who settle their scores by a shootout. The due process of law is depicted as unable properly to handle these Wild West criminals. In modern versions of the narrative, as in the movie *Dirty Harry*, bullets dispense justice. Again the ideal of a legal process is trumped.

In the May 2, 2005, issue of *Newsweek*, rocker Ted Nugent proclaimed his preferred method of criminal justice at the convention of the National Rifle Association. He bluntly stated, "Remember the Alamo! Shoot 'em! . . . I want the bad guys dead. No court case. No parole. No early release. I want 'em dead. Get a gun and when they attack you, shoot 'em." The idea of restorative justice, apparently, has never entered Nugent's mind. Swift revenge is his formula.

The same attitude appears to be permeating the sports world today. Once it was a shame to sit in the penalty box during a hockey game. Now it seems to be an honor—if the penalty was for a powerful punch to an opponent's face. Basketball was considered a non-contact sport; now when tempers burst, we see fists fly. Fines may be levied, but these violent incidents are played and replayed on TV news. Baseball and football have seen a similar increase in violence, and the crowds seem to love it.

Our highways were intended as safe and comfortable avenues of transportation, and they mostly are. But irritability and impatience have created road rage, through which some drivers justify killing or wounding who have annoy them on the highway.

Once, while at a refuse disposal facility, I was stunned by a driver who came into the yard, screeched to a halt, jumped out of his car, and began to beat the man in the car beside mine. I stepped out to ask what was going on, and the bully walked away. He had bloodied the face of his smaller victim, and that was what he had wanted to do. When the victim was asked why this man assaulted him, he said, "I guess I cut him off when I entered the road." He admitted being in the wrong, but the bruises and broken glasses seemed an undue penalty.

I took the license plate number of the assailant. When I got home took it to a neighbor who was a police officer. The officer took the side of the assailant: "That creep got what he deserved." Violence won again.

A more tragic story came from Stockton, California, in the 1990s. A teacher was shot as she drove along the city street. She had noticed that an approaching car had not put on its lights yet, and it was now dark. So she signaled the driver by a blink or two of her headlights. The young gang member wheeled his car around, drove up beside her, and shot her. At his trial he made the defense, incredible as it sounds, that "she failed to show me respect."

On a trip to China in 1984, we offered an invitation to some new friends to come to the U.S. to visit us. They responded courteously, but the woman noted that she would be afraid to walk the streets of the U.S. I didn't realize how bad our reputation was. We assured our Chinese friends that things were not that bad. A few of weeks after returning home from China, I was mugged in Sacramento, as I mentioned in the introduction. Yes, things sometimes are bad here.

Why does the U.S. have more homicides per capita than any major country in Europe or Asia? Because, some have said, we are a relatively young country, still in our adolescent stage of rebellious self-discovery. That doesn't seem to fit, since Canada, Australia, and New Zealand are the same age and have a much lower homicide rate than the U.S. Is it arrogance that infects the spirit? Poverty is an aspect of injustice more widespread than we are willing to admit. Is poverty a reason? What about drug addiction? What about easy access to guns? Whatever the causes, the U.S. is a land with an intensifying culture of violence.

The reference to the easy availability of guns reminded me of one of the saddest funerals I have been called to conduct as a pastor. A boy in his early teens got into a fight with a neighbor boy. He decided to settle the matter by threatening the neighbor with his dad's revolver. But the neighbor boy was stronger and in the scuffle seized the gun and shot his one-time friend. The boy was killed by a bullet from his father's gun.

Shootings at schools show both the twisted values of some of our youth as well as the pervasive availability of guns. The constitutional right to bear arms is often pushed far beyond what the framers intended. I recently heard a member of the NRA say that Americans would be safer if there was a gun in every home. Statistics show that greater availability leads to greater use. In Stockton, California, in the 1990s, a deranged man obtained an automatic weapon (with no difficulty it was later revealed) and went to a school playground. He proceeded to mow down dozens of children. Had he been unable to obtain such a weapon, such a tragedy would likely not have occurred.

In his book *Fear Less*, Gavin De Becker challenges us with these words:

> We live in a nation with its own violence epidemic, remember? In the past two years alone, more Americans died from gunshot wounds than were killed during the entire Vietnam War—ten times the number who died at the World Trade Center. Many people in other countries believe ours to be the most frightening place to live, and some startling contrasts support their view. For example, in all of Japan, the number of young men shot to death in a year is equal to the number killed in New York City in a single busy weekend. By this time tomorrow, four hundred Americans will suffer a shooting injury, and more than a thousand will face a criminal with a gun.[7]

Slavery was abolished over a century ago, yet in a 2006 PBS broadcast it was estimated that in the last couple of years 50,000 young girls were brought into our country to be made a part of the sex slave trade. Tens of thousands of other boys and girls are brought into our cities to work in sweat shops. These activities are of course illegal, but they are another form of violence operating on our shores. The gross injustice of it all has seemingly not bothered the conscience of those implicated. Violence against women continues at an alarming rate. It has been tabulated that over 450 women are murdered every month by their husbands or boyfriends in this great "land of the free and home of the brave."

What about our use of capital punishment? Statistical studies suggest it tends not to deter crime. Yet our government sees this as a just sentence for those who commit murder. China, Iran, and Saudi Arabia agree, but most Western nations no longer endorse the death penalty. Among other reasons, they have recognized the risks of putting to death someone who might later, by DNA or other means, be proven innocent.

There is also the recognition that some people can and do make radical changes in their lives. There are cases of prisoners who have changed their life's orientation, work effectively with prison staff, and inspire fellow inmates. Some have engaged in acts of repentance, which have helped heal some of the wounds suffered by families of victims. How troubling to have these people executed when they have become a blessing to those around them . The bottom line, however, is that capital punishment is state-sanctioned killing, another feature contributing to our culture of violence.

If religion was used to justify violence, as reviewed in chapter one, our culture of violence allows it to spread, and the media magnifies it. Gangs make killing a mark of maturity. An angry driver feels entitled to punish an offender. The strong feel they have the right to exploit the weak. Mobsters exploit children and young people for profit. Whether the profit motive or a perversion of values has spurred violence, it has taken a terrible toll in our land and in our world.

Some have called the U.S. a Christian nation. Our violence is one factor that disqualifies us from that description. Furthermore, no nation can claim to be a Christian one, since the New Testament sees the Christian church as comprised of people from every tribe and nation. Christianity can only be international. But some of our founding fathers hoped that we would behave in ways that harmonized with Christian morality. We applaud their idealism. We would be blind to deny the influence of Jesus' way in many situations. Thankfully countless thousands in our country do take seriously the love for neighbor command. Some even recognize that this includes the enemy and calls them to go the second mile.

Religion doesn't do it. Our culture doesn't do it. However, the Bible tells us of one person who did it. He is sometimes called "The Prince of Peace." But first of all he is known as Jesus of Nazareth. He identified violence as an aspect of the way of the world, part of the darkness of this world. His followers were said to be not of this world—but while in this world they were to be "light" to show a better way, a heavenly way to live even on earth: God's way of love.

In the next chapter we turn to how Jesus lived this way. How did Jesus face the violence of his day? What would Jesus do if mugged? What if he had been abused as a child? What if he had been assaulted by a Roman soldier? We cannot definitively answer such questions, but studying how Jesus did react to the violence of his day gives us important clues. Here we come to the heart of what the Bible really says about loving the enemy.

Chapter Three

We Are Moved by Jesus' Identification with Sinners

M ANY FINE TEACHERS AND PHILOSOPHERS have set forth inspiring ideas and lofty goals but failed to live them. No one reaches perfection, but the stretch toward it is recognized as honorable. When we see in someone a harmonious consistency between what is said and what is done, we are seeing a person of integrity. Jesus radiated integrity. In Jesus we can accurately interpret what he said by what he did, or what he did by what he said. Since actions speak louder than words, we will begin by looking at some of Jesus' actions and responses that give us insight into how he practiced love of enemy.

If we are to find peace with another person, group, or nation, we first need to have some understanding of who they are and what drives what they say and do. Are they hurting? Do they feel threatened? Have they been ostracized? Have they suffered unjustly? Do they lack freedom? To relate well with another, some measure of understanding must first happen. We need to step into another's shoes—or sandals or bare feet. That's how Jesus lived among us.

His identification with the lowest and the least began in the surprising details of his birth. Jesus began his life as a *Mamzer*—Hebrew for "silenced one" or "bastard," since his mother was unmarried when she became pregnant.[8] Mary would be guilty of adultery and her child considered illegitimate. Joseph, who had been considered an honorable member of his community, would lose that honor and be disgraced by marrying Mary. He would become a *Tsadig*. This stigma would be with Jesus throughout his boyhood. He would understand what it feels like to be ostracized.

Because it was known that the German language was spoken in our home, we were identified, by a few, with the enemy during World War II. I recall being called a "dirty German" by some neighbor kids; it did not feel good. Was Jesus called a "bastard" by any of the kids in his neighborhood? If so, how would he have responded?

Jesus' life began near the bottom of the social scale. His public ministry similarly was accompanied by full identification with sinners, when he went to the Jordan River to be baptized by John. Sinners were being called to repent, and when Jesus stepped forward to receive baptism, John, sensing a special holiness about Jesus, hesitated. But Jesus insisted (Matt. 3:15). His solidarity with sinners would be demonstrated from day one at his birth, years later at his baptism, and finally at his death by crucifixion, a punishment reserved for those considered the worst criminals.

In categories of class or profession, Jesus could identify with laborers; he was a carpenter. He could identify with scholars; he was a rabbi, or teacher, and his knowledge of the Hebrew Scriptures was profound. He was never rich materially. He had to remind a would-be follower that the "Son of man has no place to lay his head" (Matt. 8:20). But he understood the temptation of wealth and power as the world's riches were offered him if he would just compromise his mission (Luke 4:5-7). His clearest identification was with the poor, whom he called "blessed" (Luke 6:20).

Reflecting on the life of Jesus, the writer to the Hebrews declares that Jesus as our high priest is able to sympathize with our weaknesses, because he is "one who in every respect has been tested [tempted] as we are, yet without sin" (Heb. 4:15). The writer again affirms his identity with us in the statement that Jesus "learned obedience through what he suffered" (Heb. 5:8). Jesus understands our humanity. He's been there.

I'm always glad to hear that. This means he experienced puberty as I did. How did he look at the girls in his neighborhood? Was he tempted to watch them bathe? What did his rabbi teach the Bar Mitzvah class about sex? Jesus felt the urges of testosterone as other young men do. Jesus might have experienced sexual temptation or the inclination to hit a kid who annoyed him. If so, I'm thankful. I have felt those urges, and now I believe that Jesus understands and apparently coped with those trials.

Jesus' ministered among all kinds of people, healing the sick, and proclaiming good news of God's kingdom for all. It was this inclusiveness of Jesus' gracious contacts that scandalized the religious leaders. A holy person does not enter the home of a Gentile, talk to a woman in public (especially not one of dubious reputation), touch a leper, dine with tax collectors, work on the Sabbath, nor allow a prostitute to kiss and wash his feet (Luke 7:38-39). Jesus broke the code of religious prejudice by doing all of those things and more. The Pharisees and scribes grumbled saying, "This fellow welcomes sinners and eats with them" (Luke 15:2). He not only "eats with them" but at one wedding party he miraculously increased their wine supply by over 120 gallons after they had run dry! (John 2:11). The charge against him: "He is a friend of tax collectors and sinners" (Luke 7:34). And most of us are thankful he is.

Jesus broke through every ethnic, racial, or national prejudice of his day. Samaritans were looked down upon, so Jesus made a Samaritan the hero of one of his most memorable stories (Luke 10:29-37). The Romans were the despised foreign occupiers of Israel's land, but when a centurion requested aid from Jesus, the centurion's servant was not only healed but the Roman was praised for showing more faith than what Jesus had found in all Israel (Matt. 8:10).

When Jesus takes a brief vacation in the region of Tyre, a woman whose daughter has a serious problem of convulsions confronts him and asks for his help. There are various ways to interpret the complexities of this passage, which could be read as portraying a Jesus who is at first rudely dismissive. But one possibility is this: He sees the strength of her faith. Knowing that Syrians were called dogs by the Jews, he jests with her, using the label *dogs* ("doggies" in Greek) as a gentle test. She sees the twinkle in his eye and responds positively as Jesus expects, saying, "Sir, even the dogs under the table eat the children's crumbs." Then Jesus says, complimenting her reply, "For saying that, you may go—the demon has left your daughter." Her daughter was healed (Mark 7:24-30).

Every person who came to Jesus for help was accorded the dignity deserved by those he called "children of God." When Jesus taught about God, he nearly always referred to God as "Father," "Your Father," or "our Father," or *Abba*, a secular term for father, recorded about 190 times in the Gospels. It would be like "Papa" or "Daddy," which makes everyone sisters and brothers in one family, the family of God. As an aside, it is well to note that abba, when used by a child, is hardly a sexist term suggesting the male. It is a word that implies parental love with strength to protect and wisdom to guide.

When Jesus gave the prayer many of us learned early in our lives, he pointed out that we are to use the plural in all of our petitions: "Give us," "Forgive us," "Lead us," "Deliver us." This prayer underscores our mutual responsibility toward one another. I cannot pray "give us this day our daily bread" without remembering my sisters and brothers who are without food, and doing what I can about it.

Harmony in this family of God begins with a recognition of each person's value. "All are precious in his sight." Jesus gave that honor to each one, whether Nicodemus the Pharisee, Levi also known as Matthew the tax collector, Peter the fisherman, or the Samaritan woman who had been married five times (John 4:18). The poor and those who received the least honor in their society were the ones who received Jesus' special recognition.

In developing a new church, some of us were reminded by the conference speaker of "the homogeneous principle." Start out by gathering together likeminded people with similar social and ethnic backgrounds so they can function well together. When we observe Jesus, we see that he did *not* follow that principle. He identified with those the religious establishment rejected. The history of the church, which is to be the body of Christ, does not often demonstrate that openness. Philip Yancey faced expulsion from the fundamentalist church in which he grew up because he voiced doubts about some of its doctrines. Others have been excluded because of race, sexual orientation, social standing, prison record, or other reasons. We do not see such exclusionist tendencies in Jesus.

Notice the diversity in the disciple group Jesus assembled. The most extreme differences are seen between Simon the Zealot on the one hand and on the other Matthew the tax collector, whom most Jews would consider a traitor because of his collaboration with Rome. Jesus' choices must have seemed strange to some of those called earlier. Can you imagine what Peter might have felt when Jesus called Matthew? Maybe he mused, *It was risky enough to include hot-tempered young men like John and James, skeptics like Thomas and Nathaniel, not to mention a fanatic like Simon the Zealot so ready to kill tax collectors and Romans. But if we add the traitor, Matthew, our Zealot might slit his throat.* That was the way Zealots, right-wing extremists, operated.

But Jesus took his whole crew to eat and drink at the banquet Matthew prepared. It would be intriguing to have heard what these two political enemies, Matthew and Simon, said to each other. But they were all included in the fellowship of those whom Jesus said would be known for how much they "love one another" (John 13:35). The miracle is that, as historians have noted, they did become a group who were described as those who truly did love one another.

Maybe we have a clue here as to how to bridge animosities between people. There is something mutually affirming in dining together. In the 1980s Joyce and I were guests in

China on a month-long cultural exchange. During those times of eating and drinking, sharing art, and laughing together, we grew to love our hosts. Hal Lindsay in his book, *The Late Great Planet Earth* had called them the "Yellow Peril." We couldn't dream of thinking of them as a peril or wanting to kill them. They were family now. Bruce Chilton, in his book, *Rabbi Jesus*, goes so far as to say that Jesus replaced the baptism of John the Baptist with the communal meal, as the ritual symbol of cleansing and sharing in the "coming kingdom of God."[9] The inclusiveness of all different people around one table beautifully depicts the kingdom of heaven here on earth as well as a taste of heaven to come.

Mary Magdalene is another person any religious leader concerned about reputation would not have befriended. Jesus healed her of possession by "seven demons" (Luke 8:2). Whatever that meant, it had to have been a terrible affliction. In her gratitude and love, she became one of Jesus' most devout followers. The authenticity of her devotion was revealed in her being last at the cross and first at the tomb on the day of Jesus' resurrection (John 20:1). There Jesus commissioned her as the first proclaimer of his resurrection victory, the message she was to take to his disciples (John 20:17). (We invite those opposed to women in ministry to note that the first person commissioned to share the good news was a woman!)

Two thieves were crucified beside Jesus, and they were guilty of more than stealing. The Roman authorities would have considered them terrorists. One thief, sensing Jesus' innocence, asked to be remembered. Jesus immediately responded, "Today you will be with me in Paradise" (Luke 23:43).

Those who came to Jesus with a question, an appeal for mercy, a request for healing, or an entreaty for another were not turned away. Jesus did not question anyone's right to come to him based on racial, national, ethnic, cultural, sexual orientation, social, or religious affiliation criteria. Only those who rejected such inclusiveness—usually the religious teachers—had trouble with Jesus.

A fundamental teaching of Christianity is that all persons are sinners. All have fallen short of God's ideal (Rom. 3:23). This lack of virtue, however, does not nullify human value. All are of inestimable worth (John 3:16, Peter 3:9). To make clear to everyone that each is included in God's love, Jesus lives out an identity with the lowest and the least. He begins and ends his life in what his culture would call a disgrace. He can empathize with all sufferers because he has been there. His love, however, includes both the sufferers and those, who in their blindness, cause the suffering. We see Jesus as God's "Prince of Peace" for all people.

At this point some thoughtful Bible student might question other comments Jesus made, such as when he said of the Pharisees that "you are from your father the devil" (John 8:44). Yes, Jesus did say that. He also on one occasion called Peter, one of his favorite disciples, "Satan" (Matt. 16:23). This kind of hyperbolic language was not uncommon among prophets of that day. Jesus' references to the devil and Satan in such situations point to the source of arguments against Jesus. What such people were saying was not in harmony with God's will; it came from a "lower" source. We will cover more about that in the next chapter.

For now we recognize that the overwhelming body of evidence depicts a Jesus who was friend to the friendless and champion of the poor. His full identification with those who suffer helps us to recognize the empathy he could feel for others. When we likewise feel such empathy for those considered "enemy," then we cannot vilify or dehumanize them. They too are Jesus' sisters and brothers made in the image of God. They too are our sisters and brothers.

Seeking to practice what we preach, as we pondered Jesus' inclusive love, Joyce and I looked at each other. We named those we disliked the most. Hesitatingly yet sincerely, we prayerfully affirmed them as our own sisters and brothers and asked God's blessing upon them.

Chapter Four

We Are Impressed by How Jesus Faced His Enemies

PEACEMAKING MUST BEGIN WITH a validation of the other person or nation. So we have seen how in the inclusive embrace of Jesus, all people are affirmed as precious in God's sight.

What can we do, however, when we affirm but the enemy denies human worth? How do we face oppressors who seem unwilling to attempt dialogue? The idea of not resisting an evildoer sounds cowardly. Turning the other cheek seems totally inappropriate. What did Jesus do? His actions in the face of danger help us to understand what he taught.

So now let us notice how Jesus faced threats. He challenged the congregation at a synagogue service in Nazareth by reminding them of God's grace toward a widow of Sidon and a leper from Syria. This generated an angry response. In fact, the people were "filled with rage . . . drove him out of town, and led him to the brow of a hill . . . so they might hurl him off the cliff. But he passed through the midst of them and went on his way" (Luke 4:28-30) . They were angry because Jesus took the lesson from Isaiah to show that God's blessings are intended for Gentiles as well as Jews, even for foreign widows and lepers. That set them off. Who was this

Jesus? Was he not a carpenter? What right did he have to claim Yahweh's love for Gentiles?

Then Jesus became a possible victim of mob violence, but somehow they were unable to hurt him. How he "passed through the midst of them" we cannot say. We know he did not strike at any. He faced them. There must have been some kind of amazing authority in his stance and look. They did not, could not, kill him. That would happen later, but only when he allowed it.

A bitter encounter with the religious leaders was recorded by John. There Jesus charges that their murderous intentions are from the devil. They in turn accuse Jesus of being demon possessed. Jesus does not get physical with them, but he does challenge them: "Which of you convicts me of sin? If I tell the truth, why do you not believe me?" (John 8:46) That is a good question. We would all do well to ponder our answer. They prepare to stone Jesus, and he walks out of the temple area, probably shaking his head in anger and sorrow.

The angriest outburst of Jesus, as recorded by all four gospel writers, involved his visit to the temple during the period of Passover celebrations. This was a time when pilgrims from all over Israel would come to Jerusalem to participate in this holy remembrance of their Exodus from Egypt many years earlier. They would need all the appropriate supplies for the necessary ceremonial sacrifices—wood, oil, a bird or animal. The court of the Gentiles, the outer area where Gentile believers were otherwise permitted, was where the moneychangers set up shop. There they accepted the Greek or Roman currency, trading it for temple currency, deducting the half-shekel temple tax and, when they thought they could get by with it, gouging pilgrims with extreme exchange charges.

Jesus looks at an area of the temple once sacred to Gentile believers, now occupied by the noisy din of bankers, merchants, sheep, and cattle. He recalls the prophetic words, "My house shall be called a house of prayer for all the nations" (Isa. 56:7b, Mark 15:17). Incensed by the injustice of it and the exploitation of a sacred festival, Jesus fashions a whip of cords to drive out the sheep and cattle (John 2:15). He uses his own arms and legs to overturn the tables of the money-changers, sending them scurrying.

They probably returned to business a few hours later, but Jesus had made his point. He rejected their injustice and exploitation. He killed no one, but he made a loud and clear statement of his protest. "Turning the other cheek" did not mean for Jesus ignoring problems. Those who participate in protest demonstrations, challenging injustice, can find inspiration and encouragement from this action of Jesus.

Jesus also faced armed adversaries. When the soldiers of the high priest, led by Judas, come to arrest Jesus, he steps forward to declare he is the one they are looking for, the one Judas (whom Jesus had called "friend") has kissed (Matt. 26:50). Peter attempts a defense of his Lord by striking at Malchus, a servant of the high priest, cutting off his ear. Jesus rebukes Peter saying, "Put your sword back in its place; for all who take the sword will perish by the sword" (Matt. 26:52). Then Jesus says, "If you are looking for me, let these men go" (John 18:8) . Before they leave, he picks up the severed ear and restores it to the startled head of Malchus (Luke 22:51). The soldiers are confused by Jesus' courage and hesitate for a few moments to take him. Finally they leave with him as their willing prisoner.

When Jesus is questioned by the high priest about his teachings, Jesus challenges him to ask any of the many who have heard him, since he has said nothing in secret. That response upsets one of the officers standing near Jesus, so he strikes Jesus on the face, saying, "Is that how you answer the high priest?" Jesus does not turn the other cheek in a literal sense, but he does turn the tables on the officer: "If I have spoken wrongly, testify to the wrong. But if I have spoken rightly, why do you strike me?" (John 18:23) The officer is speechless; his unjust act has been exposed.

When Pilate asks Jesus if he is the king of the Jews, Jesus answers, "You say so" (Luke 23:4). Pilate, impatient because of Jesus' refusal to defend himself, says, "Do you not know that I have power to release you and power to crucify you?" Jesus replies, "You would have no power over me unless it had been given you from above" (John 19:11). Pilate is stunned. He has never heard a comment like this before.

In the previous chapter, we noted that in all of his associations with various people, Jesus never belittled or excluded. Here we have noted that, in the face of hostility, he did not strike opponents or take lives. Nor do we see him in cowardly retreat from an enemy. Nonresistance means, for Jesus, nonviolent resistance. In each case he faces his foes and challenges them to consider what is true. The principle of seeking to overcome evil with good is at work here. That, we believe, is the biblical way of confronting an enemy.

One thing we do not see in these encounters is a Jesus "tender, gentle, meek, and mild." He may well have conducted himself in such a manner when he was with the children or the oppressed, but when it was an enemy, he faced that person with unflinching courage and a resolve to have that person experience justice. Justice always precedes peace. Yet he did so without resorting to violence. He was always ready to accept personal suffering rather than inflict it.

However, we do not believe he would have simply stood by watching if, for example, if a child or his mother was being abused. He had harsh words for those who would mislead a child. He often defended women or other vulnerable persons. His concern for justice and mercy would lead him to defend those in peril. How he would do this, we can only guess, but that he would defend them physically, if necessary, seems possible. Just punishment is consistent with his teachings and actions. But we do not believe he would kill.

Mahatma Gandhi, committed to nonviolence as he was, conceded that there may come times when there is no other option except a violent defense that may even kill an assailant. He stressed that this would have to be the very last resort. But Jesus did not leave that option open.

We are glad to have a police department in our city. I doubt we would want to live in any town or country that did not provide police protection. The apostle Paul recognized the value of authorities that protect law-abiding citizens and punish wrongdoers. He saw these authorities as God's servants to keep order in society "If you do wrong, you should be afraid, for the authority does not bear the sword in vain! It is the servant of God to execute wrath on the wrongdoer" (Rom. 13:4).

So we acknowledge the need for police intervention, at home or abroad, by local, national, or international agencies. We see the possibility of distinguishing between wars, including against terror, considered wrong, and police actions carefully targeted to restrain particular wrongdoers. It is one thing to launch a "war on terror" viewed as justifying nearly any military action, including the horrors such action have brought Iraq. It is another thing to engage, for example, in police action to restrain particular terrorists.

At the same time, we urge all authorities to respect the dignity of human life as they fulfill their demanding tasks. Governmental authorities have been notorious in their disrespect for human dignity. Christians are called to challenge such evils. An Episcopal priest and personal friend who had heard a lecture on social ethics by John Howard Yoder shared with me a Yoder comment he would not forget: "Subordination does not mean compliance." We agree. We are to support and obey our governing authorities in so far as their mandates do not call us to disobey our higher authority. Jesus calls us to render to Caesar only those things that are Caesar's. God is first always. So while a sinful society will require police action, we do not believe Jesus would sanction the violence of killing or the tragedy of war.

With our advanced scientific knowledge, surely we can develop weapons that could instantly stop a suspected criminal without killing him or her. Too many teenagers and innocent people, as well as those who were guilty, have been killed by police action. For justice to prevail, this must not happen. The Jesus way calls us to "restorative justice" not "vindictive justice" as is inferred by killing.

We don't have guns in our home, but if I saw anyone threatening to harm a loved one, I think I would resort to using any means available, if words failed. I believe there are priorities with reference to those we are to love. God is first. Our immediate family must come next, since by marriage and having children we take the responsibility of love to guard and protect family members from all ills, as best we are able. So if a baseball bat were handy I might use it, with prayer and pleading, the purpose being to prevent hurtful actions but not kill. I would hope to remind myself that the assailant was still my brother or sister, and if possible, I would aim to communicate that. Would Jesus use a baseball bat to protect his mother or a little child? We can't know. But whatever he chose, it would be the best option.

In the next chapter we will study teachings of Jesus which will further clarify some of the actions just described.

Chapter Five

We Are Inspired by What Jesus Taught About Love

WHAT THE BIBLE BEST SAYS ABOUT loving the enemy is most clearly communicated in the teachings of Jesus. As John says, Jesus is "the Word of God" (John 1:14). When we hear from Jesus, we are hearing from God. Matthew recorded some of the most memorable of Jesus' teachings in what has traditionally been called "The Sermon on the Mount." He begins this section by quoting nine statements of Jesus, each beginning with "Blessed are..." (called Beatitudes). Among these affirmations are blessings pronounced on the meek, the merciful, and the peacemakers.

By meekness Jesus was stressing an attitude of total dependence on God. The meek are those who trust God for wisdom, guidance, courage, and strength. Those who are meek are humble and teachable. They are not arrogant, thinking they know it all. So in relations with others they are ready to listen and defer to a better idea. In no way does meekness suggest weakness. An attitude of meekness makes negotiation possible in matters controversial. The meek are willing to hear and learn what others are thinking and feeling. That includes listening to enemies.

Thomas Merton, a Trappist monk, saw meekness as an essential quality in those who hope for nonviolence methods to effectively resist evil. The meek seek a dialogue with the adversary, not an attempt to defeat the enemy. The meek seek the common good. Power guarantees the interests of some, but never for all. It protects some at the expense of others. Only loving meekness can attain the good for all, for only love expressed in meekness and humility can establish a communication that results in a positive outcome for all. Merton shows how meekness operates as he proposes this test: "Are we willing to learn something from our adversary? Are we willing to admit that they are not totally inhumane, wrong, unreasonable, cruel, and so on?"[10] The meek will do this, and Jesus calls such "blessed" (Matt. 5:5).

The merciful are those who have been so blessed by God's mercy that they readily share it. Luke words it simply, "Be merciful as your Father is merciful" (Luke 6:36). Of the thirty times the word *merciful* appears in the Hebrew Bible, twenty-five instances refer to God. This is also the way Allah is described in the Qur'an. In all but one of the 114 *suras* (chapters), the opening line is "In the name of Allah, the Beneficent, the Merciful." To show mercy to another is giving expression to a divine characteristic. In the New Testament, two themes emerge related to showing mercy. First, mercy extends pardon to someone who has wronged you (Matt. 18:32-34). Second, mercy extends kindness to someone in need (Mark 10:47). So the one who is merciful will not be quick to judge, condemn, or strike another. Patience and pardon, as expressions of mercy, can play an effective role in cooling the fires of anger and enabling peace.

Jesus blesses the "peacemakers" (Matt. 5:9). While this is the only use of that word in the New Testament, the concept of peacemaking appears throughout. Peacemaking refers to one who brings reconciliation between opposing parties. It corresponds to Jesus' teachings about love for enemies. Peacemakers are a living "demonstration of God's love through Christ in all its profundity . . . who, experiencing the shalom of God, become his agents establishing his peace in the world."[11] I do not believe the church has taken the peacemaking calling of our Lord seriously enough. With few exceptions, history does not show the church as an activist peacemaker in troublesome situations. Jim Wallis reminds the church that Jesus did not say, "Blessed are the peace lovers," but "Blessed are the peaceMAKERS."[12]

Jesus continues in his message to warn against anger. His hearers know that the law forbids murder, but Jesus takes the issue deeper, to the heart of the matter. Peace between brothers and sisters is so important Jesus places it ahead of religious duties. "First be reconciled to your brother or sister and then come and offer your gift" (Matt. 5:24). Reconciliation between the heavenly Father and God's children and between sisters and brothers all over the world lies at the heart of the gospel. Jesus takes the subject of reconciliation further by rejecting the course of vengeance. "You have heard that it was said, 'An eye for an eye and a tooth for a tooth,' but I say to you, Do not resist an evildoer. But if anyone strikes you on the right cheek, turn the other also" (Matt. 5:38-39). Jesus is saying that instead of striking back, surprise the adversary by arresting the flow of violence and causing a question to arise. Why did this person not hit back?

The "eye for an eye" reference was well known to those listening to Jesus. In fact, this expression occurs as far back as the Code of Hammurabi as well as three times in the Pentateuch. It was intended to set limits on retribution, to protect folks from undue revenge. There was judicial value in that phrase.

Jesus goes deeper when he says, "But I say to you, Do not resist an evildoer." Does that mean to let the guilty party get away with it? What could Jesus mean? One way to interpret the statement is to hear it as prohibiting legal retaliation against an offending party. Another interpretation, from *The Scholars Version*, translates Jesus' words as follows: "Don't react violently against the one who is evil." In other words, Jesus is not suggesting passivity but calling us to be both "assertive and yet nonviolent."[13]

When Jesus mentioned someone slapping the right cheek, he was referring to an insult by one who felt superior. Such an act used the back of the hand. The slap was intended to degrade or humiliate more than injure a person. However, the one who turned the other cheek caught the offender off-guard. Since by tradition the offender could only use a right hand, a back-handed slap wouldn't work on the left cheek. What to do? Attacking you with a fist would make you an equal. So if you turned the other cheek, you affirmed your worth as an equal without offering a violent response. Gandhi taught, "The first principle of nonviolent action is that of non-cooperation with everything humiliating."[14]

Jesus encourages the poor among his hearers to affirm their dignity as God's children. "If anyone wants to sue you and take your coat, give your cloak as well" (Matt. 5:40). Only the poor would be sued for a coat. To add your cloak as well could embarrass your accuser and shame him in court, since a poor man would be wearing little under his cloak. A similar idea is expressed in the next verse. "If anyone forces you to go one mile, go also the second mile." It was a long-standing custom of occupiers, from Persians to Romans, to force nearby individuals to carry their military gear. At the time of Jesus, this duty was restricted to one mile. A soldier who insisted on a citizen carrying his baggage farther could be disciplined for violating the military code.

Walter Wink, in his book *Jesus and Nonviolence*, clarifies this situation. He points out that when Jesus advises his hearers to offer to carry the load a second mile, he is suggesting something that would startle a soldier. What does this citizen mean by such an offer? Is he saying he is stronger than the soldier? Is he trying to get the soldier in trouble? Does he want a reward? The one who was exploited has now taken the initiative. The soldier is confronted by one showing courage and strength to challenge an injustice and to put the love for an enemy into action. The more commonly accepted understanding, of demonstrating a special generosity, is of course also implied.[15] As the children of God, we are to act and react in ways that are more generous than expected.

We come now to the heart of Jesus' teaching about love. He says:

> "You have heard that it was said, 'You shall love your neighbor and hate your enemy.' But I say to you, Love your enemies and pray for those who persecute you, so that you may be children of your Father in heaven; for he makes his sun rise on the evil and on the good, and sends rain on the righteous and on the unrighteous." (Matt. 5:43-45)

In Leviticus 19:18, the people of Israel are commanded to "love your neighbor as yourself." Neighbor is defined in the preceding verse as "anyone of your kin." Hate your enemy is not stated in so many words in the Hebrew Bible. It is found in rabbinical and Essenic teaching appearing in some Qumran writings, so this commandment could be expressed like this: "If one is to love one's neighbor, then the converse is also true, namely, one is to hate one's enemy."[16]

Love for family members is accepted by most people and religions. When Jesus said, "By this everyone will know that you are my disciples, if you love one another" (John 13:35), he could have been referring mostly to everyone in the family of faith. Certainly we are to love all Christians, hard as that may be. But our Lord's love command goes farther. God sets no limits to those we are to love, so enemies are included.

Love for enemies refers both to personal political or religious enemies. "It is precisely this teaching that sets off Jesus' love commandment from the Old Testament," observes the New Testament scholar Robert Guelich.[17] It is also distinct from all the other major religions, says Guelich. Jesus provides the basis for this command as rooted in a bond with God as the heavenly Father whose lavish love includes enemies. God allows sun and rain to bathe both the righteous and unrighteous. God's grace revealed in Christ radiates divine love especially for "enemies," for all of us (Rom. 5:8, 10). Those who love and pray for their enemies are children of the heavenly Father. That is how Jesus defines the conduct of those who truly are his sisters and brothers.

For those who claim that Jesus' teaching about loving the enemy applies only to personal enemies, not national enemies, Marcus Borg states that for any public figure to say those things in a politically violent situation, such as existed in first-century Palestine, would have conveyed unmistakable meaning. "Those closest to Jesus clearly understood his teaching to mean nonviolence. The early church for the first three hundred years of its existence was pacifist."[18]

Richard Hays reads Matthew as conveying Jesus' vision of a radical countercultural community of discipleship "characterized by a higher righteousness—a community free of anger, lust, falsehood, and violence. The transcendence of violence through loving the enemy is the most salient feature of this new model."[19]

Any of us can love those who already love us. The followers of Jesus are called to the harder task of loving those for whom it is hard to feel anything positive. This sets aside the shallow definitions of love related to spontaneous good feelings or happy emotions. God's kind of love included a cross, the sacrifice of death. That is the kind of love to which Christians are called.God's love is limitless. That is Jesus' teaching on love. And that, we believe, is the Word of God.

Mainline churches have for decades sanctioned their members' participation in war. In some countries allowance is made for the few who claim to be conscientious objectors to such military involvement. Churches generally support their members and honor their courage for their willingness to fight their country's foes. No one can deny their bravery and sacrifice. But the clear teaching of Jesus does not allow for any kind of killing, since such violates the law of love. In light of the New Testament's call to the Christian community as a whole to embody the teaching of Jesus about love, any sanctioning of Christian participation in war "is untenable and theologically incoherent," contends Richard Hays in *The Moral Vision of the New Testament*.[20]

Love for the enemy was to be the uniquely distinguishing feature of the followers of Jesus. "If you greet only your brothers and sisters, what more are you doing than others? ... Be perfect, therefore , as your heavenly Father is perfect" (Matt. 5: 47-48). *Perfect* here is not an insistence on flawlessness but a call to be a mature child of the heavenly Father.

Like our divine Parent (Father, Mother), whose all-embracing love includes everyone, enemies included, so are we to love. After all, when we were "enemies," Paul tells us, God's love was extended to us in reconciling grace (Rom. 5:10).

Love for the enemy, then, is the sign to the world that we are the children of the God, whom Jesus revealed. This teaching is crystal clear. God help us to obey.

I, Randy, first heard about Jesus' call to love our enemies at an InterVarsity Christian Fellowship camp in Canada. It was about a year after my conversion experience. Initially I responded with a chuckle to the invitation to pray for my enemies, since I could not think of any. Then the image of J. D., a junior classmate of mine, came to mind. In several rough skirmishes he had always prevailed. I disliked him. Now I felt obligated to pray for him, for God's best for him. I didn't feel like it, but as a young enthusiastic Christian, I wanted to obey Jesus. So every so often I would ask for God's blessing on my old enemy. Several years later I was surprised to meet J. D. again. Before I could think about it, I found myself greeting him warmly and engaging in pleasant conversation. Later I reflected about what had happened. My attitude toward him had totally changed. Was that a result of prayer?

I recall what C. S. Lewis said about his experience with prayer. He confessed to not fully understanding how prayer affects others but was confident of one thing: "Prayer changes me." My experience with J. D. made me agree.

Prayer is our major source of strength to love the enemy. Communion with the God who loved us while we were enemies will enable us by the divine Spirit to extend grace to our own enemies as well. I hope to do that when I pray for an enemy, be it the man who mugged me, the pastor who insulted me, or the president who disappointed me. I pray that God's grace will be experienced by that individual, that God's will shall be revealed to that person, and that all hostility will be dissolved. I pray also that I will have the grace to honestly extend pardon, whether I see that person or not.

In the next chapter we will see something about how the early church practiced this love for the enemy.

Chapter Six

We Are Challenged by How the Early Church Loved

NO ONE CAN CLAIM THAT THE FIRST CHRISTIANS were perfect. They had, like all of us, problems with their humanness and sinfulness. They argued about doctrinal interpretation and leadership qualifications as well as other issues. But one prominent factor did appear to distinguish them from their contemporaries. Jesus had said, "By this everyone will know that you are my disciples, if you have love for one another" (John 13:35). Apparently they really did. An early fragment contains the comment of an outsider who, when observing believers, said, "How they love one another."

The early church was a community. The church today, infected by the rugged individualism of our culture, is often seen in terms of individual players. We speak of our faith in personal terms, such as "my decision," "my giving," "my church." Personal responsibility is vital, of course—but Jesus emphasized family, and the church is that family called to embody the mission of Jesus. The ready acceptance of shared responsibilities for one another was a prominent feature of the church in the first centuries.

This love, this *agape* motive, prompted their unselfish sharing from the very beginning. Luke records this observation of the first believers in Acts 4:32-35.

> Now the whole group of those who believed were of one heart and soul, and no one claimed private ownership of any possessions, but everything they owned was held in common . . . there was not a needy person among them, for as many as owned lands or houses sold them and brought the proceeds of what was sold. They laid it at the apostles' feet, and it was distributed to each as any had need.

Love was also demonstrated in the breaking down of Jewish/Gentile cultural and ethnic barriers. Paul celebrates this reconciliation in these words from Ephesians 2:13-14.

> But now in Christ Jesus you who once were far off have been brought near by the blood of Christ. For he is our peace; in his flesh he has made both groups into one and has broken down the dividing wall, that is, the hostility between us.

They practiced that love, so Paul says in his letter to them, "I have heard of your faith in the Lord Jesus and your love toward all the saints" (Eph. 1:15). What was evident in Ephesus was also present in Jerusalem, Rome, Corinth, Philippi, and other areas where the church was growing.

Its growth, however, became a threat to the imperial rule of Rome. Christians refused to offer token sacrifices to the gods or a yearly pledge affirming "Caesar as Lord." They also refused participation in the army. Jesus was Lord, and love was their law of life. That excluded all killing. That was also what caused their persecution. For the first three centuries it was illegal in the Roman Empire to be a Christian. Persecution was at times terrible and other times not so ruthless, but throughout those years, it took courage to declare yourself a follower of Jesus or one of the "people of the Way," as Christians were called in some places. Yet despite all the tribulation the church had to endure, it continued to grow until it numbered over a million participants by 313 CE. Was unselfish love their driving force? Hear what historian Elaine Pagels records about this community as she quotes from a second-century church leader, Tertullian.[21]

Christians voluntarily contribute to support the destitute, and to pay for their burial expenses; to supply the needs of boys and girls lacking money and power, and old people confined to the homes . . . we do not hesitate to share our earthly goods with one another.

Many Christians went into the areas of the poor and offered help and money while they preached the good news "that class, education, sex, and status made no difference, that every human being is essentially equal to any other 'before God,' including slaves and the emperor himself, for all humankind was created in the image of one God."[22] This preaching was revolutionary. The emperor did not like to hear that a slave was his equal before God.

The New Testament had given equal status to Jew and Gentile, male and female, slave and free (Gal. 3:28), and the early church practiced this inclusiveness. Some women became ministers or deacons in the church. Note the references to women in Romans 16:1-15, including Junia's listing as an apostle. Slaves were welcomed as sisters or brothers (Philem. 16) and some became teachers in the church. Because this family of faith was practicing love and mutual respect for all, it absolutely refused to engage in violence. Their Lord had taught love for neighbor *and* enemy, and they understood that to mean they were not to resort to killing or any kind of violence. As noted in the last chapter, the early church for the first three hundred years of its existence was pacifist. Not only did Christians not kill, they declared opposition to all killing as a command of the Lord to be obeyed.

Sir Ernest Bennet, in *Christian Pacifist*, tells of a monk in Asia Minor who traveled a thousand miles to see if he could do something to stop the slaughter of human life in the Roman gladiatorial shows.

> In the middle of a fight he ran from his seat in the amphitheater and called upon the combatants to cease their attempts to kill each other. The furious spectators rushed in and beat him to death with sticks and stones. But the sacrifice had its effect on Honorius the Emporer. He is-

sued a prescript forbidding all gladiatorial combats. The evil spectacle was never held again.[23]

In his study of history, Leo Tolstoy found that the church fathers in the first centuries considered a role in the army incompatible with being a Christian. He quotes a church leader as saying, "A Christian cannot be a soldier and cannot be prepared to murder anyone he is ordered to." In the second century Tatian, a philosopher and convert to Christianity, declared that killing in war was not an acceptable exception to the law of love. "Killing in war was as inadmissible for Christians as was any kind of murder."[24]

At the beginning of the third century, the Christian theologian Origen said, "We will not raise arms against any other nation; we will not practice the art of war, because through Jesus Christ we have become the children of peace." Right from the beginning, when Jesus told Peter to put away his sword, the Jesus movement rejected the path of violence toward Rome and became "the peace party in Palestine."[25]

Tertullian (155-222 CE) put it this way: "It is not fitting to serve the emblem of Christ and the emblem of the devil.... One cannot serve two masters.... How can a son of peace participate in combat?" Cyprian, a few years later, chided his government for justifying warfare. He said, "Murder is considered a crime when people commit it singly, but it is transformed into a virtue when they do in en masse!"[26] Sounds familiar.

In the fourth century another church leader, Lactantius, made this statement, "There must be no exception to God's commandment that it is always a sin to kill a person. It is not permitted (for a Christian) to bear arms, for our only weapon is the truth."[27]

History records martyrs during this period who were conscripted into the military but refused to bear arms. The Egyptian church forbade its members to enter military service and went so far as to expel those who joined the army.

History indicates that the early church saw itself as a countercultural movement within a pagan society. Rome insisted on emperor worship. The church acknowledged only

Christ as Lord. Rome encouraged a culture of hedonistic practices. The church stressed purity in all relationships. Rome degraded slaves and women. The church honored slaves and women, declaring all persons of equal value in God's sight. Rome followed the practice of killing the enemy. The church practiced love for the enemy. The early Christians "saw themselves as already inaugurating the new order. So they refused to engage in war."[28]

Sadly, since the time of Constantine, the church has melded with most of the cultures of the Western nations in which she finds herself. It appears that the Christian community is no longer a nonviolent, loving, countercultural movement, standing in clear opposition to the materialistic, immoral, and warring ways of the nations.

In the past century, Germany called itself a Christian nation. So did Great Britain. We know what happened. The United States of America calls itself a Christian nation today. We claim in our pledge that we are a nation "under God." Christianity is thus identified with American culture instead of with the teachings of Jesus. We see "God bless America" signs everywhere. We probably don't see signs saying "God forgive America."

But maybe a better sign would read, "God forgive your church." The church Jesus had in mind was a company of people who would be characterized by radical, all inclusive love for everyone—including those called enemies. Christians would form a fellowship of committed caring people more ready to die than to kill. They would resist evil by all creative means, except violence and murder. They understood their mandate to be "overcome evil with good" (Rom. 12:21).

The early church, with all of its flaws, lived out that expectation. As Martin Luther King Jr. said, "We need to recapture the gospel glow of the early Christians, who were nonconformists in the truest sense of the word and refused to shape their witness according to the mundane patterns of the world."[29] Willingly they were ready to sacrifice their lives for their Lord in the cause of love. Martin Luther King Jr. did just that in 1968. Thankfully, others are ready to give their lives for the cause of love. With God's help, let us be among them.

Tom Fox, James Loney, Norman Kember, and Harmeet Singh, four members of the Christian Peacemaker Team in Iraq, were among them. Winning the respect of many Iraqis, they were nevertheless captured by a Muslim sect on March 9, 2006. Tom Fox was brutally killed. The others were kept in captivity for 118 days, until British soldiers freed them. They were grateful for their release but deeply saddened to learn of Fox's death. So were some Iraqis, although one was heard to comment that it was too bad Tom would not make it to heaven, since he was a Christian. But a member of the Muslim Peacemaker Team responded that he was sure Tom would go to God since "he gave his life for us." Those called enemies Tom saw as his brothers and sisters, and the impact of his witness has touched many in Iraq as it has in the U.S. and Canada and worldwide.

In the next chapter we will address a problem we all struggle with: the contamination of prejudice. What does the Bible say about this sin?

Chapter Seven

We Need to Learn How to End Prejudice

I RECALL THAT SOMETIME IN THE 1960S a seminar was held at North Park Theological Seminary in Chicago to discuss the evils of segregation and all racial discrimination. One of my Caucasian friends blurted out that he had not felt prejudice toward anyone of any race. Our more perceptive black friend said to him, "Think again. We all have our prejudices, and we won't get anywhere by denying we have them." He was right.

Another seminary buddy, a Japanese American, married a Caucasian woman. We thought that was just fine, but his folks were disappointed because she was not Japanese. Later he confided in us that some Japanese look down on folks of other races.

Such prejudice has apparently existed since the days of the Tower of Babel, when the sudden sound of many different languages brought confusion upon the earth. When the children of Jacob (Israel) found themselves slaves in Egypt, they experienced firsthand a racial prejudice that would haunt them for centuries. After their redemption from Egypt, they in turn put down the Canaanites and other tribes and races occupying the land destined to become their homeland. Jews and Arabs trace their hostilities back to Abraham's sons, Isaac born of Sara and Ishmael born of Hagar, Sara's slave girl.

In the last century we witnessed the terrible prejudice of the Aryan supremacy doctrine as it surfaced in Hitler's Germany during the 1930s and 1940s. Inspired by this prejudicial belief, the Nazis killed about six million Jews and thousands of others who tried to protect them in what we remember as the Holocaust.

Our own country, supposedly founded on the principles of equal rights for all, denied those rights first of all to the conquered Native Americans. Then equality was denied to the African-Americans, brought over as slaves and exploited as such for over one hundred years. Even after the Emancipation Proclamation issued by President Lincoln, the prejudice of whites against blacks persisted until the 1960s, when desegregation was finally established as the law. It nonetheless still remains in the hearts of many today.

It took even longer in South Africa to break the barriers of apartheid. In both of these countries, much of the credit for overcoming these prejudices must be attributed to the nonviolent resistance pressures led by leaders like Martin Luther King Jr. in the U.S and Archbishop Desmond TuTu and Nelson Mandela in South Africa.

More recently we have seen the 1990s "ethnic cleansing" of the Bosnians by the Serbians. Then came the 1994 genocide in Rawanda of the Tutsis by the Hutus. The same heartbreaking crisis has occurred in Sudan and continues in tragic proportions in the Darfur area in the twenty-first century. It doesn't seem to stop.

Whether they be Jews or Arabs, Protestants or Catholics, Sunnis or Shiites, blacks or whites, Hindus or Muslims, Russians or Americans, it appears that racial, religious, ethnic, national, or class prejudices exist all over the world. Why is this?

There appear to be at least four causes of prejudice: pride, insecurity, the tendency to generalize, and a failure to respect others as sisters and brothers in the one family of God.

The problem of pride becomes obvious when one group considers itself better than the other group: We are superior; you are inferior. We build ourselves up by putting the others down. We list our achievements and note the other's failures. Arrogantly we boast of our strengths and accomplishments but carefully avoid even seeing our own weaknesses. Pride is the problem dating back to Adam and Eve. There in the garden, the temptation is to become like God. When parents pass on this myth of superiority to their children, it is easily believed. Then, sadly, we may hear kids say, "There goes that dirty ⎯⎯" or "Watch out for that ⎯⎯." Arrogance is most often the problem those in power in any country.

Insecurity is also a factor in prejudice. We tend to see differences as threatening. This produces fear. Someone else's achievement or approach may be better than our own. That puts us on a lower rung of the importance ladder. Then if the other group, or nation, is higher or stronger, we may feel afraid. Thomas Merton once commented that he believed the root of war is fear.

Did America fear that Iraq might have weapons of mass destruction, which might be used against it? Was this one reason the U.S. launched its war against Iraq? Feeling cornered or threatened, we fight back with insults, violence, or any negative barrage, for "we are better than they are." We have prejudged the situation and because of our insecurity must label "them" as worse. Dialogue between equals then is impossible.

Another ingredient in prejudice comes from uncritical generalizations. We encounter rudeness in a Paris train station—then declare that all French people are rude. We were once cheated by a Korean, so all Koreans are cheaters. When we were in China in 1984, we were thought to be rich, since it was believed that all Americans are wealthy. Generalizations go on and on, labeling all people of the same race or country as having the flaw detected in some.

Surely it is not too hard to recognize that even if a few persons of the same race have caused several negative events, that does not make all people of that race guilty. We need to remember that a balance of good and bad is present in all of us, and that mutual respect is our calling from the One who made us all members of one human family. If there were aliens in outer space looking at our planet, wouldn't they call us all "Earthlings"?

Jesus confronted the prejudices of his day headon. Romans were the hated occupiers and Samaritans were the unclean heretics, so Jesus praised the faith of a Roman and made a Samaritan the hero of one of his best stories. The customs of that day mandated not touching a leper or eating with tax collectors—so Jesus touched and healed lepers and ate and drank with publicans and sinners. It was not considered a decent thing for a man to talk with a woman in public, so Jesus not only spoke with women in public, he even let a prostitute kiss his feet while a guest on Simon the Pharisee's patio. Jesus broke all of the prejudices of his day, affirming that God equally values all people. The early church for the most part followed his example, as noted in the previous chapter. Paul caught this inclusive spirit of his Lord when he wrote that "there is no longer Jew or Greek, there is no longer slave or free, there is no longer male and female; for all of you are one in Christ Jesus" (Gal. 3:28).

In our day and in our country, Martin Luther King Jr. had strong credentials to speak about prejudice. He suffered unjust beatings and incarcerations defending the rights of his people. Here are thoughts he penned while in a Georgia jail. He was pondering the statements of Jesus about overcoming prejudice by loving your enemies. He felt personally the difficulty of following this command from his Lord, but the more he prayerfully pondered it, the more he became convinced that "Love even for enemies is the key to the solution of the problems of our world. Jesus is not an impractical idealist, he is a practical realist."[30]

King begins by stressing the need to forgive as a necessary step toward reconciliation. He reminds us that "an element of goodness may be found even in our worst enemy." Remembering that God loves all people makes us less prone to hate anyone. To hate an enemy multiplies hate. "Hate cannot drive out hate; only love can do that."[31] Furthermore, harboring hatred damages the soul of the one who hates. It destroys one's objectivity and sense of values. Love is the only avenue that can transform an enemy into a friend. King quotes the often-repeated words of President Lincoln, who when asked how he would deal with his southern enemies replied, "Do I not destroy my enemies when I make them my friends?"

As King's sermon nears its climactic ending, he calls upon his congregation to face their bitterest foes with the kind of love he expresses in these words:

> We shall match your capacity to inflict suffering by our capacity to endure suffering. . . . Do to us what you will, and we shall continue to love you. We cannot in all good conscience obey your unjust laws, because non-cooperation with evil is as much a moral obligation as is cooperation with good. Throw us in jail, and we shall still love you . . . But be ye assured that we will wear you down by our capacity to suffer. One day we shall win freedom, but not only for ourselves. We shall so appeal to your heart and conscience that we shall win YOU in the process, and our victory will be a double victory.[32]

Martin Luther King Jr. was assassinated by someone who had not allowed God to enable him to cope with his prejudice. Sadly, there are still millions like his assassin. They are insecure, afraid, blind to the beauty of the diversity in God's good creation. They cling to their own narrow ways, boasting that theirs is the only right way.

As artists, Joyce and I have been amazed again and again by the diversity of God's handiwork. Every flower, every butterfly, every animal, every cloud, every person, every part of nature, is a distinctive wonder! Would we want to see all flowers white? We need to look again and see the beauty in the diversity of God's creation. Prejudice is a terrible blindness. Can this blindness be healed?

When we are melted and molded by the grace and love of God, the answer is yes! Millions will attest to the wonderful transformation that God's Spirit works in hearts open to divine love. In the capacity to love even our enemies is found the greatest freedom. Martin Luther King Jr. was in prison when he wrote much of the sermon from which these quotations were made. He was imprisoned, but he was free. His dream is being realized. With that kind of commitment to love, we can hasten its fulfillment.

Here is a pledge of nonviolence originally developed by Martin Luther King Jr. A friend of ours, and an ardent peace activist, Cecilia McKean, brought it to our attention. She said it was an adaptation of the pledge which Martin Luther King had his protesters sign before their strike in 1963 in Birmingham, Alabama. Joyce and I are seeking to follow its guidelines.

PLEDGE OF NONVIOLENCE

1. MEDITATE daily on the teachings and life of Jesus.
2. REFRAIN from personal violence of fist, tongue, or heart—in our homes, in our churches and in our world.
3. REMEMBER always that confronting violence means to seek justice and reconciliation—not victory.
4. WALK and TALK in the manner of love, for God is love.
5. PRAY daily to be used by God in order that all people might be free from violence.
6. SACRIFICE personal wishes to advance freedom from violence for all people.
7. OBSERVE with both friend and foe the ordinary rules of courtesy.
8. SEEK to be of service to others and to the world.
9. STRIVE to be in good spiritual and physical health.
10. FOLLOW the lead of Jesus who taught us that "Blessed are the peacemakers for they shall be called the sons and daughters of God."

A "Pledge of Allegiance" is often made to vow a loyalty to our country. The above vow expresses a commitment that would benefit both our country and our world. Let's make that pledge!

Chapter Eight

We Are Sad that Countries Still Choose the Futility of War

"WAR IS HELL," COMMENTED A SOLDIER after his return from engagement in World War I. That statement has been repeated thousands of times by those who have been to war.

But in country after country, history shows that we glamorize war. We call the combatants heroes. War offers young people a seemingly noble adventure. We celebrate battle victories with parades, sculptures, songs, and medals. We justify our involvement, often claiming God to be on our side. The enemy makes a similar claim. After the wars we erect memorials to honor the fallen, assuring loved ones that these men and women did not die in vain. The grief of the bereaved is real. How else can we bring them some comfort? It remains true, however, that war is a form of hell—one dire consequence of failing to follow the way of love.

Chris Hedges has long been a foreign correspondent. He has covered wars in Central America, Argentina, Sudan, the Balkans, Palestine, and Iraq. In his thought-provoking book, *War Is a Force That Gives Us Meaning*, he shares the sobering truth about war. He has personally witnessed how wars seduce societies, corrupt politics, destroy culture, and pervert basic human values, all the while taking a terrible toll on human life. "In the wars of the twentieth century sixty-two million civilians have perished, nearly twenty million more than the forty-three million military personnel killed."[33] Hedges points out that engaging in war on behalf of one's country makes one feel patriotic. Warmaking gives meaning and purpose to those whose lives are not clearly focused on some other worthy goal. He goes on to show that the violence of war often turns otherwise decent persons into killers and racists. He calls war "organized murder."[34]

Farley Mowat, a Canadian World War II veteran, affirmed in his own book that there "has never been, nor ever can be, a good, or worthwhile war."[35] Erich Maria Remarque, author of *All Quiet On The Western Front*, said that "the narcotic of war quickly transforms men into beasts."[36]

At this point I must insert this acknowledgement: not all military participants in war become "beasts." Many are ready to give their lives for what they believe to be a just cause. They grieve at war's carnage. They return (if they return) with a deeper sensitivity to human suffering and a renewed commitment to seeking justice and peace in our world. These brave souls deserve our gratitude.

However, we have noted that the effects are terrible for those who die or are wounded *and* for those who cause these tragedies. Many veterans will admit that engaging in bloody conflict leaves them haunted by gruesome memories of killings, even of women and children. The stress of recalling such atrocities removes all glamor from war. It also opens the door to psychiatric hospitals for many. Of course the hell of war is not mentioned in Army recruiting stations.

But we must remember what Senator Hiram Johnson said back in 1917, "The first casualty of war is truth." Remember the shallow idealism expressed after World War I that this was "the war to end all wars"? At the beginning of the twenty-first century there are many wars raging in various parts of the globe, including in Iraq the one the United States calls a "war on terror." Military contracts and arms shipments to many countries suggest our involvement in others as well.

A few years ago, I was honored to bring the message at a meeting of Church Women United, an interdenominational gathering of women who are actively involved in shaping the future for peace. Some of the following sobering statistics were shared. These are the approximate numbers of persons killed in the last century resulting from wars or civil uprisings. Here is the statistical summary:

100,000 killed in the Russian-Japanese War of 1904

1,000,000 killed in the Armenian-Turkey battles from 1906 through 1923

8,500,000 killed in World War I

20,000,000 killed in Russia during Stalin's reign of terror in the 1930s and 1940s

6,000,000 Jews killed by Nazis during the Holocaust from 1939 to 1945

5,000,000 Poles, Slavs, Gypsies, homosexuals, and disabled killed by Nazis during the same period.

54,800,000 killed in World War II

2,000,000 killed in the Chinese Civil War

3,000,000 killed in the Korean War

500,000 killed in Sudan during the last ten years of civil strife.

500,000 killed in Indonesia during the last three decades.

1,700,000 killed in Cambodia by actions of the Khmer Rouge 1975–1979

2,058,000 killed in the Vietnam War

1,000,000 killed in Bangladesh

4,000,000 killed in the Congo since 1984

1,800,000 killed in the Iran-Iraq conflict in 1980

2,000,000 killed in Afghanistan in the 1990s

1,500,000 killed in Sudan in the 1990s

900,000 killed in Rwanda in the 1990s

310,000 killed in Bosnia in the 1990s

200,000 killed in Guatemala in the 1990s

100,000 killed in the Persian Gulf War in 1991

125,000 killed in the 1990s Israel-Palestine conflicts

50,000 killed in the Chechnya-Russian conflict during the 1990s

14,000 killed in Sierra Leone during the 1990s

20,000 killed in Serbia-Kosovo during the 1990s

More numbers could be added from conflicts or battles in Pakistan, Columbia, Argentina, Chile, Nicaragua, El Salvador, Bangladesh, Lebanon, and other areas. One innocent death brings grief to our heavenly Parent. When we look at these statistics we wonder how God can allow it to continue.

Now at the dawn of the twenty-first century, it has been estimated that tens or hundreds of thousands have been killed in the war in Iraq. Most were civilians. I called the earlier figures "statistics." In fact, these are our own brothers and sisters, created in the image of God, each one a person of inestimable value. How dare we glamorize war when it claims such a horrendous loss of precious life! Among these victims are two million children killed in the wars of the 1990s. Three times that number were seriously injured. What has happened to their future?

Even though we celebrate military victories, there are no real victories in a war when the suffering caused by the war's devastation is fully recognized. Ralph J. Bunche in a 1950 article on "Man, Democracy, and Peace—Foundations for Peace, Human Rights and Fundamental Freedom," made the comment, "Who, indeed, could be so unseeing as not to realize that in modern war, victory is illusory, that the harvest of war can only be misery, destruction, and degradation.".

Elie Wiesel, the courageous Holocaust survivor, pointed out in his December 11. 1986, Nobel Lecture that "War dehumanizes, war diminishes, war debases all those who wage it." The revelation of how some of our soldiers have tortured the prisoners in Abu Ghraib prison in Iraq illustrates the truth of Wiesel's statement. These same young people would probably be acting with decency and propriety in circumstances other than the ugly scenario in which they have found themselves. War is degrading.

Martin Luther King Jr. put it well: "Returning hate for hate multiplies hate, adding deeper darkness to a night already devoid of stars. Hate cannot drive out hate; only love can do that."[37] Carl Jung warned of our tendency to become precisely what we fight. Unaware of what is happening, we tend to become the very thing we oppose. This is not newly confirmed psychology. Nietzsche is reputed to have said it before some of the recent wars erupted. He put it like this, "He who fights with monsters should look to it that he himself does not become a monster."[38] When we resist evil with evil, we are guaranteeing its perpetuation. War must be recognized as an instrument that is totally inappropriate for redressing wrongs. Treating people as enemies creates enemy-like reactions in them. This logic is firm as nails: Hate begets hate, violence triggers violence. War is never the answer.

Then what do we do about tribes or nations that are aggressive in pursuing their selfish aims? That is a difficult challenge. Humans are sinful, all of us. But we could agree on one thing—we will leave war out of our list of options. William Penn put it well when he wrote, "A good end cannot sanctify evil means, nor must we ever do evil that good may come of it. . . . " This is especially true since the amount of good that may come of it is nearly always trumped by the evil it causes.

Pitirim Sorokin, past president of the American Sociological Association and for thirty years chairman of Harvard's Department of Sociology, gives this observation:

> The World Wars aimed to improve the welfare of mankind, and to make the world safe for democracy and freedom. Instead, they destroyed about one-sixth of the most inhabited regions of this planet, killed and wounded more than one hundred million human beings, brought misery, disease, and poverty to the greater part of humanity, blew to pieces all the great values, spread insanity and demoralization, unleashed in man 'the worst of beasts,' and created an unprecedented chaos and anarchy. Instead of freedom and democracy, they gave unlimited tyranny, autocracy, totalitarianism, and universal coercion. The Korean War has utterly ruined the country of some thirty million and already has killed several millions of innocent Koreans. The net balance of these wars is quite negative: they greatly decreased the vital, mental, moral, social, and economic well-being of humanity.[39]

There has to be a better way. In *The Ways and Power of Love*, Sorokin spells out the creative power of love in individual and in social settings, showing conclusively that Jesus' call "to overcome evil with good" is both possible and effective. In fact, it is the only way to peace.

Tragically, too many world leaders, statesmen, and diplomats still believe in a peace achieved by limitless arming and pitiless crushing of the real or potential enemy. These are the policies that demonstrate the truth that hate produces hate and violence produces violence. In the "war on terror," the United States used its military might to defeat the smaller nation of Iraq and thereby incurred the hatred of much of the Muslim world. In fighting terrorists, we have become the terrorist to many in Iraq, Afghanistan, and other Muslim countries.

In 2003 a news report described how one of our own bombs went off course and killed over twenty civilians in Afghanistan, among them nine children. The reporter overheard the weeping father of five of those children mutter, "I hate Americans." Can we blame him? If he becomes a suicide bomber in an effort to kill Americans, we must understand his motivation.

War is not the way to address the wrongs in this world. Certainly, we shall have conflict. That is an ingredient of being human. But there are many ways to resolve our conflicts. War does not have to be one of them. Jim Wallis challenges us with these words: "We must stop thinking of war in terms of victory and defeat; rather, war is always a sign of failure—failure to resolve their conflicts in some more peaceful, effective, less costly, and less violent way. War should be a cause, never for celebration, but rather for grief and repentance."[40] That expression echoes the words of pope John Paul 11 who said, "War is not always inevitable but it is always a defeat for humanity."

In comments honoring the fiftieth anniversary of Gandhi's assassination, and available in the FOR journal *Fellowship* (June 1998), Mairead Corrigan Maguire said,

Is it not insanity to go on producing nuclear and conventional weapons that if used can destroy millions of people, if not the whole planet? Is it not insanity to spend billions of the people's money to produce and maintain these weapons of mass destruction, while millions of children die of disease and starvation . . . even though the world's governments have the resources and capability of ending starvation and poverty immediately?

We believe she is right.

In the following chapters we will look at peaceful ways of facing conflict that have been tried and tested and proved effective.

Chapter Nine

We Are Impressed by Nonviolent Successes

CAN NONVIOLENT ACTIONS OF CREATIVE LOVE really achieve social reforms and constructive changes that establish justice and peace? In this chapter we will look at some of the historical evidence. Walter Wink made the bold statement that "no one with any knowledge of history can ever again say that nonviolence doesn't work."[41] We'll begin with a little-known emperor-warrior who became an apostle of peace. Neither Joyce nor I had heard of him, nor had most of our friends. We found his story compelling.

Pitirim Sorokin relates this story of Asoka who came to his throne in India in 273 BC. He conquered neighboring provinces to consolidate his empire. But after his war in 261 BC, he was moved to a deep sense of shame as he saw the suffering and despair that his war had caused. Two years later he became a Buddhist monk. He began to preach and practice "the policies of goodness, mercy, liberality, truthfulness, purity, and gentleness,"[42] especially toward the conquered peoples. He is remembered for many works of charity, planting orchards, digging wells, constructing hospitals and dispensaries, and giving grants of money and other relief assistance for the poor, the aged, the infirm, and others with special needs.

Asoka's political administration established a complete rejection of war or any form of violence to settle conflict. His officials were to care for the temporal and spiritual welfare of the people. These officials were almost like missionary peacemakers. He even got involved in spreading education and the arts among his people. Dramas were created to demonstrate the rewards of virtue. The response was enthusiastic.

In terms of effectiveness, the rule of Asoka established peace in India for the remaining years of his life until 232 BC and for an additional forty years after. This made for almost seventy years of peace. Uninterrupted peace for almost seventy years is an exceptionally rare achievement in our world in any age.

It is also worth noting that in early American history, those colonies established by the Quakers and Brethren (nonviolent Christian denominations) suffered fewer casualties per capita from Native Americans than did other colonies. It was soon recognized that not all of these European settlers were interested in killing. The natives responded in kind. There was no need to kill people who would not kill you. This is a lesson from our history which we should not forget.

From the Roman Empire we heard, "If you want peace, prepare for war." That policy put in modern terms is, "peace through armed power." The last centuries have proven this approach to be bankrupt, but we continue to use it. A national leader in the U.S. was heard to say that "the way to peace is to wipe out the enemy." How sad! Or, the August 2006 issue of *Sojourners* put on its cover,"If all you have is a hammer ... everything looks like a nail." Surely that is not all we have, but the saying that "power corrupts" is apparently demonstrated again and again.

However, the past century has seen some wonderful political changes generated by nonviolent movements. Walter Wink identifies thirteen nations in which nonviolent revolutions effected significant changes for the better. Counting the populations of these countries, we note that they comprise 1.7 billion people, or almost thirty-two percent of the global population! Except for China, all achieved a measure of success "beyond everyone's wildest expectations."[43]

The most memorable figure of the twentieth century for demonstrating the effectiveness of nonviolent resistance to injustice and oppression is Mohandas K. Gandhi. He held no government office. But by prayer, fasting, and nonviolent actions, he became the prime mover in the struggle against Britain for independence of the world's second-largest nation, India. Gandhi's commitment to nonviolence began in South Africa. He moved there in 1891, after accepting a position in law practice for a Muslim company in Transvaal, Union of South Africa.

What awakened him to the ugly prejudice of racial discrimination, which included Indians as well as black Africans, was what happened to him on a train ride through Natal. He had bought his ticket for a first-class compartment and soon after he was seated was asked to leave because his skin color was brown. He left the train and spent a cold night in a station meditating. It was there he felt led to do something to eradicate racial prejudice, and so it was in southeast Africa that he launched his first nonviolent attacks against racial injustice. He made a personal commitment to poverty and celibacy (he already had four sons) and developed what is called "Satyagraha" or soul force, also described as a "quiet, irresistible pursuit of truth." Later in 1926, he would write, "Truth is the only goal we have. For God is none other than Truth. But truth cannot be, never will be reached, except through nonviolence." Truth and love are the words which Gandhi repeatedly uses for God.[44]

While in Africa, Gandhi led several protests against racial injustice and spent some time in jail for his efforts. Also while there, he began a correspondence with Leo Tolstoy, from 1909 to 1910, that had a profound influence on his life. He called himself "Tolstoy's humble follower." He named a cooperative farm for civil resisters "The Tolstoy Farm." They shared many of the same ideas about the doctrine of nonviolence and the dangers of Western "progress." But Gandhi turned those ideas into actions and saw them work.

Gandhi returned to India in 1915 and gave leadership to various movements of peaceful non-cooperation with the

British courts, stores, and schools. Again he found himself imprisoned by the British, but a six-year sentence became only two years when he was released for an emergency appendectomy in 1924.

One of his most memorable strikes was in 1930, when he led several thousand marchers over 241 miles in twenty-four days to the coast. There Gandhi picked up a handful of salt to protest the British taxation of all salt used in India. The next year that taxation ended. Gandhi also took up the cause of the untouchables, the lowest in the caste system. He called them "Harijans," or children of God.

When independence finally came to India in 1947, Gandhi refused to participate in the celebrations because Muslims and Hindus continued to fight with one another. He went to Calcutta amd began a fast "to end only if and when," he said, "sanity returns to Calcutta."[45] Muslim and Hindu leaders did respond with a promise of peace. He had opposed the separation of Pakistan from the rest of India and as he prayed for unity in India, on January 13, 1948, a Hindu editor of an extremist newspaper shot and killed this great man of peace.

He was once asked if he was a Muslim, Hindu, or Christian. He replied that he was all three. His God was the God of truth and love. Walter Wink, like all authors who study the heroes of nonviolence, gives us these words from Gandhi which echo, in part, the message from Tolstoy, which came from the teaching of Jesus:

> So long as the spirit of hate persists in some shape or other, it is impossible to establish peace or to gain our freedom by peaceful effort. We cannot love one another, if we hate Englishmen. . . . Love among ourselves based on hatred of others breaks down under the slightest pressure. The fact is, such love is never real love. It is an armed peace. . . . War will only be stopped when the conscience of humankind has become sufficiently elevated to recognize the undisputed supremacy of the Law of Love in all walks of life.[46]

Gandhi continued to be optimistic but recognized that to achieve a just peace by nonviolent methods, one must be more willing to be killed than to kill. To love is the most difficult way, but it is also the only way. It is heartening to see people with the courage to practice this love.

It has sometimes been argued that Gandhi's methods of nonviolent protest succeeded because the British culture was more sensitive to justice and human values than are some others. Would nonviolent methods have been effective against the unjust cruelty of the Hitler regime? Nazi Germany is often cited as a prime example of an ultimate refutation of nonviolence. Only military aggression could have stopped Hitler, many believe.

But such an argument fails to see the bigger picture. Historians wonder if after World War 1 there would have been a World War 2 had the Marshall Plan been offered Germany instead of the vindictive Treaty of Versailles. But even after Hitler came to power, some nonviolent protests were amazingly successful. Ron Sider and Richard Taylor describe a Bulgarian example. There the Orthodox Bishop Kiril challenged the Nazi authorities not to attempt the deportation of Bulgarian Jews to concentration camps, or he would lead his people in a campaign of massive civil disobedience.

The Nazis tried to pursue their anti-Jewish policies only to be met by huge street demonstrations. Thousand of letters and telegrams were sent protesting the anti-Semitic measures. The clergy even offered Jews a temporary status of "converts to Christianity" to save them from arrest. Jews were hidden in many homes of their neighbors. The bishop himself said he would lie down on the railroad tracks in front of any train taking Jews out of Bulgaria. As a result of these non-military efforts, nearly every one of the Bulgarian Jewish citizens was saved from the Nazi death camps![47] Similar stories could be told of nonviolent measures taken in Denmark, Norway, Sweden and Finland that saved the lives of thousands of Jews.

The real tragedy was that the church in Germany did not rise up in massive protest against the evils it saw happening all around. The issue here is not that nonviolence failed to work but that nonviolent protests were not used often enough and by more people.

Until we began research for this book, we had known little about the successful nonviolent revolution in the Philippines in 1986. By the late 1970s, the Marcos regime had deteriorated badly, causing widespread suffering among the people. Struggles here and there to redress injustices were quickly and cruelly repressed. Most churches opted to remain passive. Young idealists joined guerrilla movements like the New People's Army. This revolutionary band increased in popularity until it was active in about two-thirds of the provinces. That caused an increase in bloodshed and the fear of looming civil war.

Then some of the churches felt the conviction to try something better. They contacted a couple of members of FOR, Hildegarde and Jean Goss-Mayr, inviting them to come to the Philippines to consider the possibility of developing a well organized, coherent, nonviolent resistance to the unjust ways of those in power.

An influential politician, Nino Aquino, had been struggling about what his role should be in addressing the evils around him. Should it be armed revolution? Or was there a better way? After meeting with Jean and Hildegaard, he was convinced to throw his weight behind a nonviolent approach, even though questions remained.

Then began a series of seminars and workshops on the ways and means of nonviolence. Bishop Claver organized one with a group of bishops. Other groups included labor union members, students, politicians, church people, priests, nuns, and folks of various vocations.

At first there was some hesitation about working together with certain groups. Then Father Jose Blanco, a Jesuit priest, led in the celebration of the Holy Eucharist, and had one group serve another and affirmed their unity in Christ. It was a special moment for all. Their first assignment was to learn how to let God deal with their anger and resentments. They prayed to have all thoughts of violence removed from their hearts, "the Marcos within," some called it.

This movement grew under Father Blanco's leadership and came to be known as the "Movement of Peace and Justice." During their first year they held forty seminars in thirty provinces. By 1985 they had trained several hundred thousand persons in the methods of nonviolence. Their first major challenge was to guard the ballot boxes in the coming election. Reflecting on what happened, Hildegaard states,

> Young and old, men and women, priests and lay people, stood unarmed around the urns that held the ballots in the face of armed agents who came to steal them . . . It makes a great difference, in a revolutionary process where people are highly emotional, whether you promote hatred and revenge or help people stand firmly for justice, without becoming like the oppressor. You want to love your enemy, to liberate rather than destroy him.[48]

Radio Veritas, a Catholic station, was also a big help, broadcasting messages from the Gospels and from ministers like Martin Luther King Jr. They urged the troops to refrain from shooting the people. "Refuse to obey unjust orders," they proclaimed. When a reform group within the army split from Marcos control, he ordered the dissidents to be crushed. Radio Veritas called upon all listeners to fill the streets where the army was advancing and stand in front of the tanks, speak to the soldiers, give them flowers and hugs, and urge them not to kill their brothers and sisters. Several hundred thousand filled those streets for the whole weekend and kept the army from assaulting the soldiers who had left to join the peace party. On the fourth day of this outpouring of people power, the Philippine dictator Marcos went into exile. A new government was elected.

It took intense training for a year and a half to be ready for that day. That momentous accomplishment was not a "lucky happening," as one paper called it, but the result of prayerful planning and careful preparation. This is a model for others to study when they are striving for liberation against an unjust oppressor. Could we not teach courses in our seminaries and churches on how to conduct nonviolent demonstrations for worthy causes?

Former president Jimmy Carter has demonstrated this kind of discipleship in the work of the Carter Center. This organization of peacemakers has waged peace by monitoring elections in numerous countries, enabling citizens to choose their own leaders in a democratic process. Hope for a better future has been brought to many by conflict resolution initiatives, which avoid all violence. Farmers in Africa are trained to improve their agricultural methods thus providing healthy food for thousands. Several million have benefited from some of the Carter medical programs that are eradicating the Guinea worm and river blindness. These excellent programs provide a great example of fulfilling the biblical mandate to "overcome evil with good" (Rom., 12:21).

In the news we read of the unforgettable contrasting reactions of two fathers. One father in Afghanistan looked at the remains of his burned children killed by one of our "smart bombs" and said, "I hate America!" Suppose another father, in an African nation where the waters have been made drinkable by the efforts of the Carter Peace Center, looked at his beloved children, no longer potential victims of West Nile virus. Might he not feel gratitude rather than hatred toward America?. Turning an enemy into a friend is still the best way to defeat evil.

The best-known North American nonviolent activist was Martin Luther King Jr. Here was a Christian preacher who acted out his sermons on liberation. After Rosa Parks was arrested for violating the segregation seating ordinance for public transportation, King participated in a year-long boycott of the buses in Montgomery, Alabama. In 1957, the Southern Christian leaders Conference elected King president and their efforts doubled the number of black voters.

The following year, King and his wife Coretta visited India at the invitation of Prime Minister Jawaharlal Nahru to study the nonviolent methods and successes of Gandhi. After returning to the U.S. in 1960, King became his father's associate pastor at Ebenezer Baptist Church in Atlanta, Georgia. That same year he initiated a sit-in movement to protest the discrimination at lunch counters. It gained success as others joined it, and it spread to South Carolina, Tennessee, and Virginia. It was then that he helped form the Student Nonviolent Coordinating Committee, or SNCC.

As efforts at desegregation continued in buses, stores, restaurants, and voting opportunities, violence did break out from time to time. King always rejected that reaction. In 1961, after a bloody encounter with the police in Albany, he called for a "Day of Penitence."

In 1962, King led workshops on nonviolence, but the hostility of the southern whites was intense. King was jailed and 959 teenagers were arrested for protesting school segregation. A tragic outcome of some of the violence was the death of four little girls due to the bombing of a black church.

King continued to preach and lead nonviolent protests. In 1963, he led 125,000 people on a Freedom Walk in Detroit, Michigan. In August that year, 250,000 black and white folks gathered for the Freedom Walk in Washington, D.C. It was there that he delivered his famous sermon, "Let Freedom Ring."

Finally in 1964, King proposed a march from Selma to Montgomery, Alabama. Governor George Wallace refused a parade permit. Those who gathered to march, about 500, were beaten by the state troopers. But hundreds of black and white supporters joined in the march and after four days, about twenty-five thousand supporters greeted them when they reached Montgomery.

In 1965, King was awarded the Nobel Peace Prize, and *Time* magazine featured him on the cover as "Man of the Year." His vision for justice and peace was expanding when, in 1967, King opened a new chapter in his struggle against oppression by voicing strong opposition to the war in Vietnam. He was opposed to the use of violence of any kind as a tool for resolving conflict. When a riot broke out in Memphis by frustrated young blacks, the reaction of the police was swift and bloody. On April 3, 1967, Martin Luther King Jr. gave an emotional appeal to reject the use of violence adding, "no matter what might happen to me." The next day he was shot and killed. Until her death in 2006, King's wife, Coretta, continued his ministry of spreading hope through efforts of justice and peace.

For King, there were moments of deep discouragement, and days of pain from beatings and imprisonment. But by God's Spirit, he gave his life for the way of love. He practiced what he preached. His legacy will not be forgotten, and we pray that the barriers of segregation and racial injustice will continue to radically decrease. Nonviolent actions of love have yielded considerable success.

Martin Luther King Day is now a national holiday. May we remember what was accomplished and how it was achieved. We pray that the ministry of reconciliation will continue year after year in our country and throughout the world.

Chapter Ten

We Are Inspired by Stories of Nonviolence in Action

*T*HE CHALLENGING ACCOUNTS of Gandhi and Martin Luther King Jr. have made worldwide headlines. We have seen in their leadership the positive results of nonviolent resistance to prejudice and injustice. But too often we look at their successful engagements as rare exceptions. We are not convinced that nonviolent approaches will always work.

The fact is that nonviolent actions will not always work, if by "work" we mean some immediate success. There will be some heartbreaking costs to pay. In 2003 Rachel Corrie, at age twenty-three an American peace activist, tried to save some Palestinian homes in the Gaza strip. As an Israeli bulldozer approached, she stepped in front of it, waving it to stop. It didn't. She was crushed to death. The army later described the incident as regrettable but criticized the protester for acting irresponsibly.

However, it must be stressed that there are Jewish, Muslim, and Christian peacemakers who strongly believe that the alternative to nonviolence is always a worse option. The choice of love as the guiding motive for all actions is made because it is the right choice and therefore the best choice—not because it always works in some pragmatic way. Convinced that the way of love is the best option, a disciple will make that commitment and leave the results with the "Author of Love and Life."

We believe the following stories will warm your heart.

Pitirim Sorokin, founder of the Harvard Research Committee in Creative Altruism, in his classic work, *The Ways and Power of Love*, shares at least a hundred stories of how different people at different times reacted nonviolently to various serious threats. Three of his documented accounts follow.

An elderly Quaker lady was vacationing in Paris, France. Upon entering her hotel room one day, she was startled to find an armed thief rifling through her dresser drawers looking for jewelry or money to steal. Recovering from her shock in a few moments, she quietly told him to take whatever he could find. She even told him where to look since, she added, "you apparently need it more than I." Suddenly the man uttered a low cry, dropped what he had taken, and ran out of the room. The following day the hotel receptionist gave this lady a letter that someone had brought in for her. It was from the would-be thief. In it he wrote, "I'm not afraid of hate. But you showed me kindness. It disarmed me."[49]

Another case of "disarming" love is shared by Sorokin as taken from Allan Hunter in his book, *Courage in Both Hands*. Three Dutch sisters risked their lives during the 1940s by sheltering Jewish friends. When a German Gestapo man called on them, they invited him into their home. On a regular basis these sisters would take some time for evening devotions with some Scripture, prayers, and a hymn, and they asked if he would like to join them. With some initial reluctance, he began to visit with them regularly at the time of their evening prayers.

When "Jews" came up, the German showed his anger. Then one of the sisters mentioned that there is a biblical reference to God calling his people (the Jews) the "apple of his eye." That further angered the Gestapo man. He took out his revolver. The women said nothing. After a tense moment, he gave them the gun and admitted in sudden conviction, "I am a sinner." He left. They never saw him again. He would continue to be in their prayers.[50]

In 1905, the Russian Revolution caused virtual anarchy across the land. Bolshevik soldiers roamed areas of southern Russia destroying and looting everything in their paths. For anyone to believe in God and/or to own property was to be aligned with the czar—turning such a person into an enemy. Among the threatened villages were some Mennonite communities. One family heard of an expected raid coming their way, so the husband asked his wife to prepare a good meal for as many guests as they could seat around their table. The children were sent to bed upstairs.

Eventually a band of about six men banged on the door and drew their weapons. The father invited them in and told them his wife had prepared a good meal for them. They hesitated, looked around, and then, no doubt because hungry, entered and sat to eat.

Their next surprise was seeing beds prepared in the next room. They were invited to spend the night. They did. The following morning the band's leader told the father, "We have to go now. We came to kill you, but now we can't."[51] They left with a different view of their enemy and probably redirected other bands past that Mennonite farm as well.

This particular story reminded me of an experience my father shared with me. He and his family were Mennonites living in Russia at the time of the revolution. Food was scarce, so protecting the garden became an important assignment of the oldest boys. One evening my dad, then at seventeen an athletic young man, was on duty. A young soldier slipped into their garden and began stealing vegetables. My father tackled the soldier from behind before he could take his rifle from his shoulder.

Then came the surprise. The soldier simply crumpled. He was starved, "skin and bones," according to my father. My father apologized to the young soldier and invited him in for some *borscht* (soup) and *zwebak* (buns). The other family members joined in, and a potential enemy became a friend, at least for that night.

Note that I made allowance for the tackle under the category of nonviolence. This is partly because it was not an assault with a deadly weapon, but admittedly, mostly because it is my father's story. I would add, however, that defense of family and loved ones does not go counter to the principle of nonviolence. Every sinful society will require police or some similar protection, as noted in chapter 4. Killing is what is to be avoided at all costs, and there are many ways of accomplishing that goal.

My grandfather, a Mennonite minister, related a fascinating account from his time in Russia when roving bands of soldiers from the disbanded army would attack, kill, rape, and pillage the Mennonite settlements. He gathered the men into their chapel and prayed for guidance. They decided that they would all take their hunting rifles and protect their village by firing at the advancing soldiers, being careful not to hit any. The gunfire alone frightened the attackers away several times. Before they caught on, the families had left their Russian community for Canada.

In her book, *They Loved Their Enemies,* Marion Hostetler has collected twenty-six stories of how African Christians have exercised nonviolent love toward those who have hurt them in some way. The following story comes from Angola.

In an arrest of his mother, young Nsiamindele witnessed the brutality of the police in Kikaka as they whipped his mother and sentenced her to hard labor. But, tied to the back of his mother was Nsiamendele's baby sister. Surely the policeman could see her. However, during the whipping the baby girl was killed. The young boy shouted at the policeman, "You killed my sister! When I'm big, I'll pay you back for what you did to my mother and my little sister."

Some years later after both of his parents had died, Nsiamindele, now living with his uncle in Matadi, attended a Christian school and made a commitment to follow Jesus. Then came a serious inner struggle. Nsiamindele learned that the former policeman who had beaten his mother and killed his sister was living in Matadi as well. How would Nsiamindele keep his vow to kill the policeman and keep his new vow to Jesus to be merciful and forgiving? He shared his struggle with a relative, Don Manuel Mata, who also being a

Christian, reminded his young nephew that Jesus calls us to be forgiving as God has forgiven us. They made their decision. They invited the former policeman over for an evening meal.

After dinner Nsiamindele asked if the man recalled that fateful day when he whipped his mother and killed his sister. He did. Nsiamindele said, "I promised then that I would kill you for having killed my little sister. Jesus has shown me that I must forgive you instead. And I pray that God will forgive you also." The former policeman confessed his cruelty and begged for God's pardon and theirs as well. Prayers were offered by all and then tearful happiness filled the room. A former enemy had become a friend.[52]

Peggy Faw Gish of the Appalachian Peace and Justice Network authored an essay on peace studies. In it, Faw Gish records several stories of nonviolent confrontation. One that impressed me was of an older woman in Athens, Ohio.

The woman was walking home along a city street carrying two large bags of groceries. Suddenly she heard two men approach her from behind. Sensing what they were planning, she pondered what to do. Just before they were close enough to touch her, she turned around. With a grin, she thrust her packages into their arms and told them how glad she was to see them going in her direction. "I was nervous on this street," she said, "and these bags are so heavy. Would you help me?"

The men, no doubt taken aback, accepted her request. The three walked along conversing together until they reached her apartment. There the woman thanked the men, telling them they were so kind to have helped her. She entered her home with gratitude to God.[53] I have often wondered how those men felt after this encounter with their would-be victim.

Angie O'Gorman, writing on Jesus' method of enemy love, points out that Jesus wanted wholeness, well-being, and life for those broken, sick, or dead. Jesus' method of disarming evil was a response that would *decrease* evil instead of feeding it as violence does. The concern of the one attacked is to be for the safety of the assailant as well as for oneself. O'Gorman tells an amazing story of what happened to her one night in her home.

She recalls that she was suddenly awakened by a man who had entered her house and kicked open the door to her bedroom. Fear and near panic rushed through her body. Would he rape her? Kill her? Then a thought, rare for a victim, crossed her mind. Whatever happened, both could suffer to some degree or both could make it through this ordeal without serious damage. She began to engage the intruder in simple conversation. "What time is it?" "How did you get in?" She quietly explained that she was not well off financially and had very little in the way of material possessions. He said this was also true for him. After some time she asked him to leave but he said that he was homeless and had no place to go. Then, with amazing courage, she offered to let him spend the night in a room downstairs. Needless to say, she spent a sleepless night in her room upstairs. She reports that "the next morning we ate breakfast together and he left."[54]

Reflecting on her experience, Angie O'Gorman comments on how a victim can exert an influence for or against violence.

> Assailants are prepared for a response of fear, panic, or hostility. A violent response or one of terror, reinforces the assailant's expectations and sense of control. That would be playing the assailant's game. But a totally unexpected reaction causes hesitation, even wonder. "Introducing an element of wonder into the assault situation tends to be disarming."[55]

Wonder disarms. The unexpected non-threatening response throws the perpetrator off balance, and the setting of the encounter has changed. The assailant is astonished by the amazing reality that the one he was to victimize actually cares about what happens to him. Nonviolence breaks the escalating cycle of threat and counter-threat, to reverse the direction. When grace and love are allowed to permeate a meeting with an enemy, aggression loses its hold and new choices become possible.

Another story to illustrate this principle was related by Cornelia Lehn in *Peace Be With You*.[56] In 1967 Edgar Epp became the chief administrative officer (warden) of the Haney Correctional Center in British Columbia, Canada. His commitment to Christ's teaching of nonviolence led him to instruct all the members of his staff to put all guns in storage. "I do not consider guns necessary in dealing with human beings, including sentenced offenders," he said. While such was not the usual way of handling the prison job, things went fairly smoothly for the next couple of years.

Then came a crisis. It was Easter Monday 1969 when a riot broke out during the time prisoners were given opportunity for some outdoor recreation. About 130 young men broke into a garden shed; armed themselves with rakes, hoes, and spades; set fire to the shed; and demanded to see the warden. Edgar Epp had been out with his family on a picnic that afternoon. As soon as he received word about the riot, he rushed back to the prison.

Surveying the situation, he decided to walk out toward the fenced enclosure where the prisoners were shouting and throwing stones. He approached the spokesmen for the group and asked them to tell him their complaints. Some he felt were unfounded, and he told them so, but others he felt were valid. About these he would do something. The prisoners seemed surprised and grateful. That evening they noted that their warden was having supper with them, unarmed as usual. The staff often feared for his and their safety, but soon became increasingly impressed with his handling of the situation. Later he was asked to lead training sessions on nonviolent ways and methods of dealing with prisoner unrest.

We return to the Bible for our last story. He was an enemy of the church. Inspired by religious zeal, Saul of Tarsus led a persecution of the followers of the Way, killing and imprisoning many. He was present when Stephen, a follower of Jesus, was stoned to death, but something must have remained in Saul's memory of that event. Stephen had asked for God to pardon those who were killing him. Had Saul also been told that Jesus prayed for the Father's forgiveness of all who were responsible for his crucifixion? Saul was seeing firsthand that the people in the Jesus movement, like their master, forgave their adversaries, didn't kill them.

This conviction reached a climax on the road to Damascus, when he heard a voice from above saying, "Saul, Saul, why do you persecute me?" When he asked who it was, the answer came, "I am Jesus whom you are persecuting" (Acts 9:4-5). At that moment the one whom Saul considered an enemy he discovered to be his gracious friend, extending to him pardon and the commission for a great assignment.

Saul, meaning "big one," became Paul, meaning "little one," for Jesus was now the true "big One," Lord and Savior. It was grace that turned an enemy into a devout friend and follower of Jesus. Paul was not punished for his sins. Jesus had taken care of that. But he was called to spread the wonderful news of God's lavish grace to folks all over the Gentile world. He is still recognized as the church's most effective missionary.

Violence feeds on violence. The above stories are only a few of thousands that could be told to show how the reactions of loving nonviolence have brought healing and hope in otherwise desperate situations. The question we are left with is this: Are we ready to commit ourselves to nonviolent reactions to those who threaten us? We have been the recipients of amazing grace. How can we not share it?

Chapter Eleven

We Are Moved by the Redemptive Role of Forgiveness

JOYCE AND I HAVE BEEN WORKING TOGETHER on this book from its inception, sharing ideas and stories, editing and critiquing what we have written. Joyce is the one who usually tells me to lighten up when I get too academic. She will remind me to try to share a negative subject in a positive way. When it came to a chapter on forgiveness, Joyce asked if she could write it on her own, knowing full well that it would involve significant personal pain, since this is an area in which she has struggled for many years. With this pain has come healing, a necessary ingredient in the process of forgiveness. Here are Joyce's thoughts on forgiveness.

Shortly before writing an earlier draft of this chapter, I heard on a radio talk show that research has shown that nearly one-third of all illnesses can be directly related to *bitterness*. Other studies indicate that the percentage is much higher. We've all experienced this feeling at one time or another. It's that nasty sensation of resentment, anger, hatred, got-to-get-even that gnaws away at us somewhere in our midsection.

In these studies, the bitterness was often traced to a failure to forgive some person or persons. Surf the Internet or go to any library or bookstore, and you will find volumes of research telling us that an unforgiving spirit can result in numerous physical and mental disorders. We seem to forget that centuries of religious teachings commend forgiveness as a virtue. Now, there is scientific evidence that forgiveness is a way to a healthier, happier, and more peaceful life.

As a child, I recall that my mother would often say, "Oh, I will forgive . . . but I'll never forget!" Of course, what she meant was that she would never truly forgive the deed. As I grow older, I realize there is merit to that remark . . . but only when one realizes the need to make the memory a part of the healing process. To offer a fully conscious act of forgiving, it is important to have a clear recollection of what has happened and then to free oneself of the entrapment of that memory. Forgiveness means letting go of anger and resentment. It is a choice to not let past hurts continue to cause us more hurt.

Sometimes that may mean that we must make a renewed effort to forgive every time that memory resurfaces. If we simply recall the incident over and over to reinforce our anger or hurt, or so that we can devise ways to get even, we become victims yet again. And the pain continues. It takes a conscious effort and an act of the will to forgive. Forgiveness doesn't mean that we have to "stuff away" our anger or hurt feelings and pretend that all is well. This is like building up steam in a pressure cooker. Eventually, it must find release, and this type of letting off steam is almost always destructive.

Admittedly, I am not a psychiatrist or psychologist. My knowledge and training in this field is the result of having experienced what I consider a great wrong. I continued to be a victim for many years because I simply did not know how to forgive. I didn't understand how necessary it was for my own well being.

When I was a child, spanking was quite acceptable, even recommended by some. But my "spankings" went far beyond, crossing the line into child abuse. Perhaps worse was the verbal abuse. Until I left home at 18, hardly a week went by in which I was not told I was ugly, hateful, worthless, that it would have been better had I never been born. My mother's favorite outburst was to say that she "would like to cut your throat and watch your blood run out all over the floor."

I grew to believe that for some reason I must deserve this abuse. I must be as bad and worthless as I was told. My high school years were a nightmare of fear, lies (after all, I could never let those around me know of such a home life), and a pretense that all was well. I became a master of the cover up. I became a cheerleader, a class officer, on the homecoming queen's court . . . and everyone's friend. This was my way of proving that I was a good person, one worthy of admiration and acceptance.

When I married just out of high school, I decided I would become the perfect wife, the perfect mother. I would disprove all I had been told about what a loser I was up until that time. Ten years and three children later, I began to realize I was failing in my pretense. I was only suppressing my fears, my anger, my feelings of worthlessness.

When we hurt, some of us find that it helps to find someone or something to blame. I blamed my mother for it. I began having nightly dreams of ways to get revenge. I even had dreams of ways in which I could kill my mother. I would often awake with clenched fists, crying out curse words. I was angry and hurting so much of the time it is no wonder that the marriage did not survive.

However, during that marriage, our family had begun to go to church at the urging of a wonderful grandmotherly neighbor. It was the beginning of a long and sometimes painful journey.

Children who have been victims of violence often grow up to be violent themselves if they do not receive good counsel, support, and love as they mature. Violence is all they have seen and experienced. Though I desperately wanted to be a good mother, I would sometimes follow the way my "role model" had shown me. I was quick to slap, quick with a sharp tongue for any infraction. Then I would anguish over some act that made me feel any resemblance to my mother. The bitterness and desire for revenge for how I felt she had molded me would surface yet again.

It was not helpful that the church we were attending preached a vengeful and fearful God. Hellfire and brimstone was their message, and fun was synonymous with sin. If you sinned, you would be sent to an eternal fiery hell. The "God is Love" verse that my children were learning in Sunday school seemed phony.

I became a closet God hater—a conviction I knew I must suppress at all costs. The very thought was surely an unforgivable sin! Yet I knew I was only serving God out of fear. It was like a replay of my childhood. I said I loved God because I felt I should, I must. I would be punished . . . and this time, eternally, if I did not. I tried to convince myself that God loved me but couldn't bring myself to think that God could "like" me. In this attitude, bitterness and anger only festered. I continued to feel unloved and unworthy. Leaving my marriage became another attempt to wipe the slate clean and continue the search for love and acceptance.

After being a single parent for ten year, I married the man who would become not only my husband but also an important teacher in spiritual matters. He stood by me as my memories continued to haunt me. He held my hand when I awakened sobbing in violent anger, feeling a desire for revenge against both my mother and my church experience. Mostly, he talked a lot about God's love, grace, mercy . . . and forgiveness. Together, we read everything we could find about how people's lives had been changed once they were able to forgive or accept forgiveness. We would often read aloud to each other while traveling. I'll never forget the time we had to pull off the road so that we could weep together in joy as we read from Philip Yancey's book, *What's So Amazing About Grace*.

Each time I felt anger over some terrible wrong done to me as a child, I was encouraged to recall it, release it, and forgive it. I heard "You can't unring a bell" often. Slowly, I came to realize that I could do nothing about what had already happened. I couldn't rewrite history. I could choose to be bitter—or better. After so many years of bitter, I longed for better. And better would only come through forgiveness.

I am convinced that our choice to love, to hate, to forgive, or to seek revenge begins in our earliest years. We are prone to emulate those closest to us. If what we see is a dour expression, a hand swift to slap or abuse, a quick fit of anger in response to most any infraction, or the holding of a grudge because a lesson needs to be learned, this can all too easily be our learned reaction as well. How we express our emotions is often learned by example. Of course, through the impact of God's grace, love, and mercy in our lives, we can learn to love and forgive when we are older and more mature, but how much damage may be done before this might occur! According to the Domestic Abuse Hotline, children who grow up in a violent atmosphere are at a much higher risk of becoming substance abusers, becoming involved in abusive relationships and/or becoming violent themselves.

One evening as I watched the international news on television, I was startled to see a young Palestinian boy of about ten waving a rifle. Face distorted by hate and anger, he shouted obscenities at a group of Israelis just down the road. "I will kill you, I will kill you!" he cried over and over.

Where had he learned such hatred? The history of the strife between Israel and Palestine goes back centuries. Each generation repeats what it has learned from the one before. One side is the enemy, the other must seek revenge. Our own country's past is marred by oppression, prejudice, hatred, and injustice. The color of one's skin, ethnic heritage, education (or lack of it), social standing (or lack of it), political affiliation, sexual orientation—all are reasons for hostility.

To read the newspaper or watch television for one day is to be overwhelmed with the chaos and violence that surrounds us because of learned behavior teaching us that revenge is virtue and forgiving is weakness.

We must learn to forgive, or our world can't survive. Without forgiveness, there will be no peace. When we feel that we have been wronged by a person, event, group, or nation, our hurt and anger, left unchecked, can mushroom into violence. The perpetrator becomes our enemy; we want revenge.

I sometimes ask myself why I have reached this point of feeling so strongly the need to forgive. On a personal note, finding the ability to forgive my treatment as a child has most likely saved my mental and physical health. This is not to say that there are not still moments of sorrow because of my childhood experience. Even now, when I am in a gathering where others begin telling of wonderful memories of home and family, of a loving mother and a safe and secure home life, I feel sad that I do not share such memories. But my own memories no longer hold me prisoner, causing me to run from the room in shame and tears. An ounce of sadness is much easier to deal with than a pound of resentment.

It is only in forgiving that we break the cycle of blame and pain. Not to forgive blocks all roads to change. If we are to call ourselves Christian, we must seek to make loving and forgiving our lifestyle, not just a once-in-awhile activity. Yet I've known times when the very suggestion of forgiveness prompts actual anger in some. Once when I was bringing some thoughts from this chapter to a small congregation, a number of the people there actually shook their heads and visibly scorned such counsel. "Get real" and "naïve," several said in whispers all could hear.

A few years ago, as I watched the birth of my grandson, I found myself overwhelmed with countless emotions. Joy, of course. He was beautiful, perfect, already obviously intelligent. But I was also gripped by feelings of protectiveness, apprehension . . . and fear. Could I partner with his fine parents in teaching him to mature wisely, to be kind even to those who might be unkind to him? Could we show him by example how to be generous because it is the right thing to do? Could we teach him to laugh often, to love and respect his world and others? Could I convince him that we have a wonderfully creative God who is good, kind, and merciful even though bad things may be happening all around?

Would he come to understand that the ability to forgive others is a great virtue in an age when forgiveness is often not the politically correct thing to do?

Surely others have wished this for their children and grandchildren. Or are there those who would seek revenge for actual or perceived past wrongs through their offspring? Is the hatred and resentment so strong they cannot let go of it but feel compelled to pass it on?

Each day we are confronted with situations that call for forgiveness. In my case it was an abusive parent. I later learned how much I needed to forgive my early church experience and the damage done by what was surely very poor theology. Many occasions cause hurt, anger, and frustration. It's often easier to replay the memory and feel victimized all over again.

Is this what happens to the Israelis and the Palestinians? The Shiites and the Sunnis and the Kurds? The blacks and the whites and the Mexicans and the Asians? The Democrats and the Republicans? The heterosexuals and the homosexuals? The conservatives and the liberals? Is there no end to the divisiveness and the anguish such conflict causes?

The Hebrew-Christian Bible is rich in stories of forgiveness and its joys, its reconciliation benefits, its ability to change lives. It has not been until recently, beginning mostly in the late 1980s, that the subject of forgiveness has found favor in the secular and academic world. Lewis Smedes (author of *Forgive and Forget*), Jimmy Carter, former missionary Elisabeth Elliot, and Archbishop Desmond Tutu, who help lead a non-profit organization called "Campaign for Forgiveness Research," are among those trying to support and advance forgiveness research.

Why is forgiveness so difficult, even unpopular? Many view it as an act of the weak, the wimpy, those willing to "give in" and "give up." Forgiveness is a way of letting someone who has wronged us get off the hook, a covering up of a wrong, a mushy make-believe. Those who view forgiveness this way may choose instead of forgiving to live an event over and over—and the wound never heals. Retaliation seems to be the more desirable path. Some feel that it is not only their right to get even but even their duty.

Who will stand up and say "I'm sorry? I forgive"? It may not—no, it will not—be easy. How can we find the strength to forgive acts that are so hurtful?

I will always remember reading the book *The Hiding Place*, by Corrie Ten Boom. Whenever I'm having a particularly difficult time forgiving, one of the stories from that book comes to mind. Corrie had survived the Nazi concentration camp but her beloved sister, Betsie, had not. Betsie had been unable to withstand the terrible punishment and torture inflicted upon the prisoners by many of the S.S. guards. Corrie could only watch as her dear sister became weaker and weaker until she died.

When Corrie was finally free, she returned to Holland and began to preach throughout the area about what God had come to mean to her throughout her ordeal. While preaching at a church in Munich, Germany, she spotted a former S.S. guard from the camp where she and her sister had been held. All the suffering inflicted by this man immediately played out once again in her mind. She felt a deep sense of revulsion . . . even hatred.

When the message ended the man came forward to thank Corrie for her words. She hesitated. Then her own story that she had just related ran through her mind. She said a quick and fervent prayer, asking God to give her the strength to extend the grace of forgiveness. In the next instant she was shaking the guard's hand. To her surprise, she felt love and compassion stream from her heart to this man she was greeting. You can read more of her amazing experience in her book co-authored with John and Elizabeth Scherrill.[57] When we are called to love our enemies, we discover that God gives us the grace to do so.

Sometimes I try to imagine what our world might be like without forgiveness. It quickly becomes my worst nightmare. What if every child who had ever been abused continued to carry that grudge forever? What if the blacks could never forgive the whites and the whites could never forgive the blacks? What if every country that had ever been conquered only relived the past humiliation and dreamed of ways to get revenge? Why forgive the guy who cuts me off in traffic, the doctor who damaged my baby, the obnoxious neighbor who always lets her dog poop on my lawn, the used car salesman who sold me a lemon . . . or the Iraqi—or the American—who shot my son?

I am not suggesting that we just sweep it all under the rug or pretend it never happened. Forgiveness doesn't mean that we throw justice to the winds. People need to be held accountable for their actions. However, in trying to hold persons accountable, we all too often respond with the Old Testament teaching of "an eye for an eye." But God, as revealed in Jesus, shows us a more excellent way. It is called *grace*—undeserved favor. God's way is that we love one another and forgive one another. Amazingly, this is to include the enemy! This is God's radically inclusive love.

Does this mean that the police officer should smile at the murderer, the drug user or dealer, the spouse or child abuser, the violent sex offender and meekly say, "I forgive you"? Of course not! But *how* we hold people accountable will ultimately determine the fate of all people everywhere. We call our prisons "correctional institutions," but do we actually help prisoners correct their behavior?

If our response is violent, then the "law of the harvest" will hold true. Violence will sow violence. If our response to an angry outburst is another angry outburst, we only continue the cycle of anger. If we do not like how another country is ruling its people and we take it upon ourselves to militarily impose upon them what we're sure is a better way, the right way, a vast number of those people will feel exploited and want revenge—violent revenge. Evil cannot be crushed by more evil. Instead, evil only perpetuates evil.

So, what is the answer to the dilemma that faces our increasingly violent world? I wish I could say that in the struggle to experience forgiveness in my own life I have learned easy-to-follow guidelines, something to be written on a card and carried in a wallet. I have read volumes on forgiveness, yet aside from becoming convinced that I must strive to be a more forgiving person, I have not found any magic solution, any quick fix to what is in fact the burden of my heart.

I can only say that I have tried it and it works. I can point to the message of forgiveness by so many others who will testify to the wonders that have been realized by those who have been willing to forgive. I, and we, need to take time to read some of the statements of Martin Luther King Jr., Mahatma Ghandi, Jimmy Carter, Louis Smedes, Nelson Mandela, Leo Tolstoy, and so many more. Yet the list will never be nearly long enough.

In *What's So Amazing About Grace*, Philip Yancey states that forgiveness is an "unnatural act" and goes on to say that "the only thing harder than forgiveness is the alternative."[58] No one can force another person, group, or nation to forgive. We can only hope to set an example by being one who is willing to stand and say, "I'm sorry" or "I forgive." Let it begin with me.

Chapter Twelve

We Are Challenged by the Biblical Call to Justice and Peace

WE ALL LOVE THAT WORD *PEACE*. We long for the day when "they shall beat their swords into plowshares, and their spears into pruning hooks" (Isa. 2:4). And war shall end. Peace is a common biblical theme. The word *peace* is a greeting (Col. 1:2), a fruit of the Holy Spirit (Gal. 5:22), a command (Rom. 12:18), and an age introduced by the Messiah who will be called "Prince of Peace" (Isa. 9:5).

There is, however, one condition that the Scriptures regularly mention: no peace without righteousness or justice. Isaiah foresaw the time when God's Spirit would be poured out—"then justice will dwell in the wilderness, and righteousness abide in the fruitful field. The effect of righteousness will be peace" (Isa. 32:16-17).

My uncle, Peter Dyck, conducted numerous missions with the Mennonite Central Relief Committee in Europe after World War II. Having personally witnessed gross injustices, he often made the statement that there can be no peace without first of all establishing justice. That is the biblical order.

That was the vision expressed by Augustine in his *City of God*, in which where he affirmed that justice "and justice alone is the only possible bond that can unite humanity." Scholars have found 1,060 references in the Hebrew and

Greek languages for justice in the Bible. Here are a few of those references.

Referring to God, Psalm 89:14 emphasizes that "righteousness and justice are the foundation of your throne." Nehemiah acknowledges that God has been "just in all that has come upon us" (Neh. 9:33). The messianic reference in Isaiah speaks of one who will establish his kingdom "with justice and with righteousness" (Isa. 9:7). In the last book of the Bible, the songs of praise extol the God of justice. "Great and amazing are your deeds, Lord God Almighty! Just and true are your ways, King of the nations!" (Rev. 15:3). In her book *Bible of the Oppressed*, Elsa Tamez states that "Yahweh is the manifestation of justice."[59] And because our God is just, those created in the divine image are called upon to be just. The following are a few such calls.

Note the commission to Abraham: "I have chosen him that he may charge his children and his household after him to keep the way of the Lord by doing righteousness and justice" (Gen. 18:19). Justice is "the way of the Lord" and it is to be, therefore, the way of God's people. "To do righteousness and justice is more acceptable to the Lord than sacrifice" (Prov. 21:3). This theme is repeated by Micah, who phrases it powerfully: "He has told you, O mortal, what is good; and what does the Lord require of you but to do justice, and to love kindness, and to walk humbly with your God?" (Mic. 6:8).

Because the mandate of justice is so central to how God's people are to live, it was the special responsibility of the kings and leaders of the people to use their authority for justice. Even the Queen of Sheba recognized the role of a king in Israel. She says to Solomon, "Because the Lord loved Israel forever, he has made you king to execute justice and righteousness" (Kings 10:9).

The kings of Israel were not always just, but in this prayer we hear the cry for each to be: "Give the king your justice, O God . . . May he judge your people with righteousness and your poor with justice. . . . May he defend the cause of the poor of the people and give deliverance to the needy" (Ps.

72:1-4). As the theme of justice unfolds, the poor and needy are mentioned more and more. "Give justice to the weak and the orphan; maintain the right of the lowly and destitute. Rescue the weak and the needy; deliver them from the hand of the wicked" (Ps. 82:3-4). Kings and all leaders of the nations will do well to heed this wisdom, "By justice a king gives stability to the land, but one who makes heavy exactions [taxes] ruins it" (Prov. 29:4). Thus says the Lord God, "Enough O princes of Israel! Put away violence and oppression, and do what is just and right" (Ezek. 45:9).

So we see that Hebrew law equates the service or worship of Yahweh with the service of one's fellows. Duty to God was not confined to the religious realm. It had to do with political and social life as well. As the Decalogue had already made clear, to worship the living God meant conveying honor and respect toward others. "You shall not murder. You shall not commit adultery. You shall not steal. You shall not bear false witness against your neighbors" (Exod. 20:13-16).

Isaiah was a prophet who understood that God is far more concerned that his people do justice than that they conduct religious ceremonies. This is how he heard God speaking:

> "I cannot endure solemn assemblies with iniquity... your appointed festivals my soul hates;... I will hide my eyes from you even though you make many prayers, I will not listen, your hands are full of blood. Wash yourselves; make yourselves clean; remove the evil of your doings from before my eyes; cease to do evil, learn to do good; seek justice, rescue the oppressed, defend the orphan, plead for the widow." (Isa. 1:13-17)

Jesus addresses this longing for justice as he quotes from Isaiah in the synagogue at Nazareth,

> "The Spirit of the Lord is upon me, because he has anointed me to bring good news to the poor. He has sent me to proclaim release to the captives and recovery of sight to the blind, to let the oppressed go free, to proclaim the year of the Lord's favor." (Luke 4:18-19)

The "year of the Lord's favor" is when the poor receive the good news, when the enslaved are set free, when the blind see and the oppressed go free. When Jesus says "Blessed are the poor" (Luke 6:20), he is referring to material poverty. Too often we have spiritualized that saying using Matthew's reference, "poor in spirit" to suggest that Jesus meant only those who recognize their moral poverty. That thought is included, but the poor in the Bible are those who are hungry, helpless, and humiliated by the oppression of the rich and powerful. The poor are those who lack the wherewithal to live full and healthy lives because the resources for such have been snatched away by the injustices of those in authority over them. The year of the Lord's favor is a time when society as a whole, not just a few individuals in it, will rejoice in righteousness and justice for all.

Peace then is not just the absence of war, but the actualization of just social relations among all people. The Hebrew word for peace, *shalom*, includes far more than peace of mind. It refers to communal well-being in which God's justice reigns supreme. Shalom is a fulfillment of the often repeated petition in the prayer Jesus gave us, "Thy will be done on earth as it is in heaven." When God's will is done on earth, a heavenly harmony, the divine shalom, transforms selfish people into a caring, cooperative community of justice and love.

The United Church of Christ is one of several denominations taking seriously Jesus' call for "peacemakers." In a strong appeal to their constituency, they published a book entitled *A Just Peace Church*, edited by Susan Thistlethwaite. Here is how the biblical vision of shalom is described from this book. "Shalom means wholeness, healing, justice, righteousness, equality, unity, freedom, and community. Shalom is a vision of all people whole, well, and one, and of all nature whole, well, and one."[60]

Injustice destroys the possibility of peace because, in its varied forms, all injustice is a type of violence. When the rich oppress the poor, this is an expression of violence, Dehumanizing the helpless is another form of violence. Enslavement or exploitation of laborers is a crippling form of violence. Sexual violation of women and children is another terrible form of violence. All injustice takes various violent shapes against humanity.

So the true peacemaker not only resists participating in warfare but also embarks on every possible course of action to identify and condemn these forms of injustice. The peacemaker actively participates not only in stopping these forms of violence but also in planning and actualizing a better way of addressing difficult situations.

The widespread poverty in our world is not just a social and political issue. It is a profoundly moral and spiritual concern that ought to tug at the heart of every Christian. How can anyone not be moved in learning that eight hundred million people around the world are malnourished and, according to the World Health Organization and UNICEF, 30,000 children die every day in poorer countries from hunger and preventable diseases. Nearly half the world lives on less than $2 USD a day and 1.2 billion of them live on less than $1 a day.

The hearts of Millard and Linda Fuller experienced that tug, but not until a personal crisis led them to make a renewed commitment to the way of Jesus. Then they gave away most of their million-dollar savings and moved into a cooperative housing project, called Koinonia Farms in Americus, Georgia. It was designed and led by Clarence Jordan, a godly social activist for the poor. The Fullers lived there for over four years and during those days caught the vision of love in action. Later they would call it the "theology of the hammer."

Moved by the millions of people who live in sub-standard housing conditions, millions in the U.S. alone, they felt inspired to begin a venture that would help those in need to build and own their own decent and affordable homes. They began their work in the Congo in 1973, then after returning to the U.S. in 1976, they began the ministry of Habitat for Humanity International. This worldwide nonprofit organization in 2006 had housing minisries in 99 countries, including the U.S., and has partnered with needy families to build over 200,000 homes. In 2007 they were building a new home somewhere in the world every 24 minutes. After the tsunami disaster around the Indian Ocean in 2004, Habitat responded with the building of 25,000 smaller houses to meet the emergency. It has been a joy for me to serve on a Habitat committee and learn more and more about their great work around the world.

Studies show that poverty and infant mortality are directly linked. In the March 2005 issue of *The Covenant Companion*, John E. Phelan Jr., asked why, if we truly believe in the sanctity of life, "do we not care for it as much after the birth as before?" World Vision is one of several agencies that have demonstrated a wonderful holistic care for children in need around the world. Literally hundreds of thousands of children have been lifted from desperate situations to better health, education, and wholeness through the efforts of this Christian ministry.

A true peacemaker is consistent in taking a pro-life position—opposing all injustice and violence against the unborn and the born. For us, this means rejecting capital punishment and opposing all wars as well as any lethal forms of violence. This is not only because of a conviction against killing, but because there is a better way to challenge injustice and evil. The apostle Paul described it in 1 Corinthians 13:13, "The greatest of these is love." And love always attempts to overcome evil with good. That is the biblical way of confronting the enemy. That is God's way! Let's also make it our way.

Chapter Thirteen

We Ask, Could We Have Chosen a More Excellent Way After 9-11?

COULD WE HAVE CHOSEN A MORE EXCELLENT WAy **after 9-11?** In this chapter Joyce gives her response to that question.

Few of us in America will ever forget where we were on September 11, 2001. At the time, Randy and I were living in the sleepy little town of San Andreas nestled in the Sierra foothills of northern California. People were always asking those who lived there if we lived on that famous San Andreas fault line. Finally, a banner was designed for our one major street that said, "San Andreas . . . it's not our fault!" We used to make jokes about how little excitement ever occurred in our tiny town and laughingly said we would almost welcome at least a small earthquake. Then 9-11 happened—and our world crumbled as though we had actually been hit by one of those infamous California quakes. The anguish of 9-11 reverberated across our country in after-shock fashion; the world as we knew it forever changed.

I'm not in the habit of turning on the television in the morning. An hour or two in the evening is about my limit. Therefore I did not witness that awful event live. I only learned the tragic news when Randy ran up our front steps returning from an early morning clergy meeting. I was shocked by the stricken look on his face. I knew immediately that something terrible had happened. Randy had recently had heart surgery, and I grabbed hold of his hands, which were ice cold and trembling. "Are you all right?"

He lifted my hands to his face. I realized that he was crying. "Yes," he said, "I'm all right. But our country isn't!"

He began to spill out the news. With the rest of our country and much of the world, we turned on our television and began to watch that terrible experience... over and over during the next few days. Eating a regular meal was unthinkable. Sleep came only when we were too exhausted or too heartbroken to watch anymore. Even in sleep, the questions would not stop. Who could have been responsible for such a destructive and loathsome act. And why?

Over the next days, weeks, and months—and now years—at least some of those questions have been answered. But to what extent we believe the answers appears to split down party lines. We have become a polarized country. Our post-9-11 presidential elections have divided family against family and neighbor against neighbor. We have become a nation of fearful people. Fear is a debilitating emotion. We feel at risk, vulnerable, violated. Too often with those feelings comes a strong desire for revenge, the need to hit back, to get even, to get them before they get us. So we flex our muscles, puff out our chest, and say we will get rid of our fear by getting rid of our enemy.

Such thinking produces a conundrum. Whom do we trust to tell us who that enemy is? What method do we use to rid ourselves of the enemy? Perhaps the most difficult question of all becomes this one: How do we respond to Jesus' command to *love our enemy*, especially in the face of such danger, fear, and vulnerability?

When things are going well, we easily give glowing testimony to trusting God in the face of all our vulnerability. Yet when real fear sets in we begin to build our arsenals. We listen to various options as to how to deal with the growing problem of terror . . . usually ending up agreeing with the one that supports what we already believe. What might be helpful discussions often become raging debates, with no opinions changed on either side. We lash out in anger and grief and end up inflicting more anger and grief. We become violent. If not actually physically violent, then at least verbally violent.

We are prone to condone such reactions by reminding ourselves that the enemy is real, the danger is imminent, the threat too great to ignore. We convince ourselves that violence is the best way out. Somewhere in the deep shadows of our mind the seed begins to grow that maybe there is a "just war" after all. If there ever was a time for violent revenge, surely this is it. Jesus' command to love our enemy soon becomes relegated to a different time and place. There are some who say that what Jesus was referring to was personal and not national enemies. Various political leaders tell us that since we are "a Christian nation" (a title not only inaccurate but no more deserved than by any other nation), then God is surely on our side. I recall reading and hearing that a number of political and religious leaders felt they had clearly heard God's call to go to war against this enemy.

We had been friends with a couple for many years before 9-11. We had worshiped, traveled, laughed, and cried together. Following the tragedy, we began to discuss how we might respond to the attack. For the first time in our twenty-year friendship, we began to realize that we did not share the same opinion on matters political and perhaps even theological. The husband felt that America had a right to hit back immediately—in fact, to obliterate this enemy. That the enemy had not yet been identified did not seem to matter. The more we tried to have a discussion about options other than outright war, the more incensed he became. His face became red, the veins in his neck popped out, and finally he screamed at us that people who didn't share his perspective "should leave this country"! Perhaps he felt better when we did move, at least from that state, soon after. We continue to pray that there will someday be healing between us.

The encounter with these friends and similar responses such as theirs has led us and others we know to question the way our nation chose to react. The attacks on New York and Washington D.C. were violent, callous, destructive, and evil. The attackers seemed to have no regard for the number of innocent lives that would be taken. We feel rage and grief at this terrible loss of life. The divisiveness it has poured out upon this country is unspeakable. So many lives have been dramatically changed and disrupted in countless ways, from how we feel when we fly in an airplane to how we react when we see someone who looks remotely like a Muslim. We don't like the feelings of fear and the thoughts of revenge that now constantly gnaw at the edges of our mind. This is one of those times when the command to love enemies is put to the test for all of us who consider ourselves followers of Jesus.

We love to have guests in our home. It has been a rule since the beginning of our marriage that wherever we live, we must have a room in our home that allows for guests to gather around a table to share a meal, dessert, coffee, tea, or a glass of wine and discuss anything we choose. Another rule accompanies that discussion. When we disagree, we must listen to each side, sometimes only arriving at the conclusion that we will simply have to agree to disagree. Admittedly, some of the discussions can get heated. Even those who profess a strong faith in God take sides on what constitutes right and wrong.

The question of what is the right or wrong way to respond to an enemy has been an urgent one since 9-11. Everyone seems to have a "could've, should've" theory. Yet although we are often divided on *how* to react, one question always seems to surface. "Why do they hate us so?" On many occasions we hear this answer; "They hate us because of our freedom." For us, this reply never had the ring of total honesty. In talking with friends and acquaintances from other countries, we find that most do not see our "freedom" as the reason for the hatred. On almost every occasion their response is that "We dislike America because of it's *arrogance* . . . that and the fact that your national motto seems to be 'might is right'!" This particular answer is a direct quote from a passenger sitting next to me on the plane as we traveled to Europe for an art tour the year after 9-11. We were to hear it many times during that trip.

In the early weeks following 9-11, the United States had the sympathy of much of the world. Many media accounts now say that we have squandered that sympathy. A majority of the world now feels no sympathy or is outright hostile toward us. Why? Could it be our becoming obsessed with hunting down and punishing the terrorists? Are we so intent on revenge we will no longer listen to the voices in our world asking for a saner, more peaceful solution? It appears that we were so eager to hit back we quickly and violently chose to invade Iraq even though no 9-11 terrorists were from that country. Our color-coded terrorist alert shifts colors seemingly without meaningful thought or reason. We have become a nation ruled by fear.

Years have now passed since that horrendous September morning. There are those who feel that we as a nation reacted badly. Others conclude that we reacted well and that we should continue on our present path. These differences of opinions have made our country a house divided against itself, splitting political parties, turning church against church, creating an almost obscene war of words within our media, alienating friends and even family.

When my children were still at that age during which they were best friends with someone one day and worst enemies the next, vowing they "would never speak to him/her again," I would often ask them to invite the "offender" over to our house. They could squirm, stick out their tongue, make faces, and be generally disagreeable. But they had to talk *and* listen to each other. Rarely did they leave as enemies.

As I think of children I am reminded of an incident Randy shared with me about his encounter with a neighbor. Randy was about twelve and ready to defend his younger brothers from all "enemies." When a younger neighbor boy hit Randy's brother, Randy took matters into his own hands and punished the neighbor boy. Soon after, Randy was confronted by the boy's dad, who told Randy that the punishment of his son was *his* responsibility, not Randy's. When we become parents, we grasp that we, not somebody else, are responsible for our children's conduct. Maybe there is a lesson here for our nation. If Islamic fundamentalists are the problem, should we not allow the "parents," the leaders of Islam, to discipline their own wayward people? If they are truly ready to embrace the peace agenda many of their leaders claim, then let *them* take the lead in punishing the terrorists. Other nations can lend support, but Muslims bear the major responsibility for teaching and leading their own people. A number of Muslim nations indicated a readiness to do this after 9-11, but we took matters into our own hands instead of working with them. Many of these Muslim nations now see the U.S. as enemy instead of friend.

In the last few years, we have been told from both sides of the political arena that we "will not talk with terrorists"! Are we, in truth, saying we choose not to *listen*? What option does that leave us? Does the fact that we will not talk or listen condemn us to be forever enemies? When confronted by an enemy, most feel that there are only two alternatives—flight or fight. As a mother and grandmother, I long for another option. I yearn for reconciliation.

In the wonderful Sermon on the Mount, Jesus tells us, "blessed are the peacemakers for they shall be called the children of God"! Wise counsel, for the history of our world shows that war, and its accompanying violence and destruction, has never brought about lasting peace. John F. Kennedy once said that "mankind must put an end to war or war will put an end to mankind!" Peacemaking *must* become a priority in our world . . . if our world is to remain. Enemy love is at the very heart of Jesus' teaching. It's not given as an option. It's a command. Reconciliation is the desired outcome of learning to love the enemy.

A woman in our town is always writing letters to the editor. Her politics and her theology are at the opposite end of the pole from mine. I find her views offensive. Every time I read one of her letters, I just want to smack her! Then I force myself to calm down and go back and actually *listen* to what she has to say. Sometimes, I even learn something. Even in small matters, when we feel we have been offended, our first thought is to hit back, retaliate, to get even. When the offense is as diabolical as the 9-11 attack, the reaction is multiplied many times over. Reconciliation has a hard time making it to our to-do list.

In Romans 12:21 we are told to "overcome evil with good." This instruction seems almost contrary to human nature. The acts of 9-11 were so abhorrent, so evil, the very thought of looking for a way to do anything "good" borders on repulsive, revolting, even impossible. Our mantra seems to be, "The only good enemy is a dead enemy." We cannot bring ourselves to look on the enemy as people created in the image of God. It then becomes almost easy to demonize an entire country. This is how we can conclude we must crush their way of life, innocents included, because of the acts of a band of zealots.

As I write, my mind wanders back to the title of this chapter. Could we have found a more excellent way following 9-11? There has been great debate over the way our government responded. In choosing to react to violence with more violence, have we only made matter worse? Even with all our military intervention, many would say we are no safer today than before September 11.

On a personal level, when I find myself searching for a better answer, I envision a leader who is a "benevolent dictator." This sovereign would choose to take war off the table as an option for settling disputes. The law of the land would insist that the rulers of what are now enemy nations gather around in a great circle. The leaders of terrorist groups would be included. They would talk ... and they would listen. They would be required to share their hopes and dreams and desires for their people. All the mothers and grandmothers of the world would be the mediators.

There would be a call for an end to poverty. All those in authority would be required to see that all nations had adequate food, housing, and health care. Distribution would be fair and equitable. At this table, we would do what the song says: We would "hammer out justice . . . mercy . . . freedom." We would do all this without violence.

As we contemplate the great command to love our enemy, perhaps the radical teachings of Jesus as stated by the apostle Paul still provide the best answer:

> Let love be genuine; hate what is evil, hold fast to what is good; love one another with mutual affection; outdo one another in showing honor. Do not lag in zeal, be ardent in spirit, serve the Lord. Rejoice in hope, be patient in suffering, persevere in prayer. Contribute to the needs of the saints, extend hospitality to strangers. Bless those who persecute you, bless and do not curse them. Rejoice with those who rejoice, weep with those who weep. Live in harmony with one another, do not be haughty, but associate with the lowly; do not claim to be wiser than you are. Do not repay anyone evil for evil, but take thought for what is noble in the sight of all. If it is possible, so far as it depends on you, live peaceably with all. Beloved, never avenge yourselves, but leave room for the wrath of God; for it is written, "Vengeance is mine, I will repay, says the Lord.' No, if your enemies are hungry feed them; if they are thirsty, give them something to drink, for by doing this you will heap burning coals on their head. Do not be overcome by evil, but overcome evil with good." (Rom. 12:9-21)

No matter how much we debate, we can come up with no better solution than this command. I have been laughed at, made fun of—even screamed at by those who say this is a naïve and childish dream. However, so far, all other methods of response in which violence plays a role have only led to more violence. Is anyone willing to stand up and give peace a chance?

Chapter Fourteen

We Are Convinced of the Supremacy of the Law of Love

*I*N THE FIRST CHAPTER OF THIS BOOK, we pointed to negative influences found in certain religions. That, of course, is not the whole story. Here is another look at what can be found in many of the world's religions. Prophets, poets, sages, and scholars from many religions and in all ages have recognized the life-enhancing role of love. You will be impressed by the similarities expressed by different religions in the following examples. These quotations are indebted to a comparative anthology of sacred texts in the volume *World Scripture* (St. Paul, Minn.: Paragon House, 1995).

Anas and Abdullah reported God's message as saying, "All (human) creatures are God's children, and those dearest to God are those who treat his children kindly." —*Islam, Hadith of Baihiqi*

"For the poor will never cease out of the land; therefore I command you, you shall open wide your hand to your brother, to the needy, and to the poor in your land." —*Judaism, Deuteronomy 15:17*

"You shall love the Lord your God with all your heart, and with all your soul, and with all your mind. This is the greatest and first commandment. And a second is like it; you shall love your neighbor as yourself." —*Christianity, Matthew 22:37-39*

"Have benevolence toward all living beings, joy at the sight of the virtuous, compassion and sympathy for the afflicted, and tolerance toward the indolent and ill-behaved." —*Jainism, Tattvarthasutra 7.11*

"Do good to him who has done you an injury." —*Taoism, Tao Te Ching 63*

"Do not be overcome by evil, but overcome evil with good." —*Christianity, Romans 12:21*

"Conquer anger by love. Conquer evil by good. Conquer stingy by giving. Conquer the liar by truth." —*Buddhism, Dhammapada 223*

"A superior being does not render evil for evil; this is a maxim one should observe . . . One should never harm the wicked or the good or even criminals meriting death. A noble soul will ever exercise compassion even toward those who enjoy injuring others of those of cruel deeds when they are actually committing them—for who is without fault?" —*Hinduism, Ramayana, Yuddha Kanda 115*

"The good deed and the evil deed are not alike. Repel the evil deed with one that is better, and lo! he between whom and you there was enmity, shall become as though he were a bosom friend." —*Islam, Qur'an 41:34*

"Those immersed in the love of God feel love for all things." —*Sikhism, Adi Granth, Wadhans M.I., p. 557*

"He whose heart is in the smallest degree set upon Goodness will dislike no one." —*Confucianism, Anolects 4.3-4*

"Compassion is a mind that savors only mercy and love for all sentient beings." —*Buddhism, Nagarjuna, Precious Garland 437*

"Let none deceive another, nor despise any person whatsoever in any place. Let him not wish any harm to another out of anger or ill-will. Just as a mother would protect her only child at the risk of her own life, even so, let him cultivate a boundless heart toward all beings. Let his thoughts of boundless love pervade the whole world." —*Buddhism, Sutta Nipata 143-51, Metta Sutta*

> Strong One, make me strong.
> May all beings look on me with the eye of friend!
> May I look on all beings with the eye of friend!
> May we look on one another with the eye of friend!
> —*Hinduism, Yajur Veda 36.18*

"Hatreds never cease through hatred in this world; through love alone they cease. This is an external law." —*Buddhism, Dhammapada 3-5*

Hillel said, "Be of the disciples of Aaron—one that loves peace, that loves mankind, and brings them nigh to the law." —*Judaism, Mishnah, Abot 1.12*

"If anyone says, 'I love God,' and hates his brother, he is a liar; for he who does not love his brother whom he has seen cannot love God whom he has not seen." —*Christianity, 1 John 4:20*

"Now faith, hope, and love abide, these three; and the greatest of these is love." —*Christianity, 1 Corinthians 13:13*

"You have heard that it was said, "You shall love your neighbor and hate your enemy," but I say to you, love your enemies and pray for those who persecute you, so that you may be children of your Father in heaven." —*Christianity, Matthew 5:43-45*

Sensitive and perceptive people of nearly all religions recognize the supremacy of love and the need to put it to work. I have never read a stronger case for practicing love than the following testimony by Pitirim A. Sorokin, which emerged from his 1818 persecution, imprisonment, and death sentence by the Russian Communist government. The government mistreated him and others in ways nearly beyond enduring but stirred him to write in his diary that

> Whatever may happen in the future, I know that I have learned three things which will remain forever convic-

tions of my heart as well as my mind. Life, even the hardest life, is the most beautiful, wonderful, and miraculous treasure in the world. Fulfillment of duty is another marvelous thing making life happy. This is my second conviction. And my third is that cruelty, hatred, violence, and injustice never can and never will be able to create a mental, moral, or material millennium. The only way toward it is the royal road of all-giving creative love, not only preached but consistently practiced.[61]

Then writing decades later, he reports that his experiences, as well as experimental studies at the Harvard Research Center in Creative Altruism he established, confirmed these truths:

Hate begets hate, violence engenders violence, hypocrisy is answered by hypocrisy, war generates war, and love creates love.

Unselfish love has enormous creative and therapeutic potentialities, far greater than most people think. Love is a life-giving force, necessary for physical, mental, and moral health.

Altruistic persons live longer than egoistic individuals.

Children deprived of love tend to become vitally, morally, and socially defective.

Love is the most powerful antidote against criminal, morbid, and suicidal tendencies; against hate, fear, and psycho neuroses.

It is an indispensable condition for deep and lasting happiness.

It is goodness and freedom at their loftiest.

It is the finest and most powerful educational force for the ennoblement of humanity.

Sorokin concludes that "only the power of unbounded love practiced in regard to all human beings can defeat the forces of inter-human strife, and can prevent the pending extermination of man by man on this planet." He is convinced that "Without love, no armament, no war, no diplomatic machinations, no coercive police force, no school education, no economic or political measures, not even hydrogen bombs can prevent the pending catastrophe." Yet he also worries how little is known about "love energy," which he observes is so absent from science, and especially human science texts, that "the word 'love' is not even indexed" in them.[62]

Sorokin needs no excuse for his contributions. His monumental work, *The Ways and Power of Love*, was released in multiple editions, the first published in 1954 and a recent one republished in 2002 by the Templeton Foundation Press as a timeless classic. Will we hear his prophetic call?

Thankfully, some scholars are addressing the issues of peace and conflict. Ralph K. White, a psychologist of Quaker background, worked for almost all of the twentieth century to show how psychologists can make a positive difference in steering the conflicts of our day toward peaceful resolution. He stressed that an essential first step toward peace is to develop a realistic empathy with the adversary—not agreement or approval, but understanding. This is one of the characteristics of real love.

Why should there not be a class on the real meaning of love and how to practice it in every elementary and high school grade? Why should it not be taught in our colleges and universities? Should not our doctors and nurses, diplomats and congressional leaders, lawyers and teachers, business executives and employees, police officers and prison guards, know as much as possible about cultivating and practicing the art of selfless love? Would it not make a big difference in our country if our politicians were required to pass such a test before they could run for office, especially the U.S. presidency?

We need to rid our minds of the idea that love is only something you feel, a pleasant sentiment associated with romance. We have nothing against *eros* or sensual love. However, the *agape* love we are considering here has to do with the will and mind of the person, far more than with his or her feelings. This love thinks, ponders, and studies that which might be the best for another person—then, difficult as it might be, puts that idea into action. We used the word *difficult.* That may be an understatement. Love can demand our life, so the commitment to love calls for courage as well as thoughtfulness. We therefore wholeheartedly agree with Sorokin's emphasis that an intense research in this field should take precedence over almost all other studies and research. Nothing less could change our world for the better. We foolishly boast of our advances in rocket science while all we can think of, for the growing criminal element in our land is more prisons. We fight terrorism with terrorism, as if that has ever worked!

Think of what might have been done with the billions of dollars the U.S. has spent on the invasion of Iraq if those funds had been used other than for warfare. Imagine if those billions had been spent on helping Muslim and other nations (as well as our own) with health care and educational needs as well as addressing human rights violations and advancing democracy.

At the time of this writing, tens of thousands or more people, including over 4,000 American service personnel, have lost their lives. Hundreds of thousands more have been seriously injured in the Iraq conflict. More are dying every day. Apparently the idea of overcoming evil with good is rarely considered.

Maybe we haven't practiced the discipline of love enough on the interpersonal level. Yet there are countless instances of actions of love have melting the anger of an antagonist, be the enemy personal or corporate. The study of history shows that in most cases, violence breeds violence, even as love gives birth to more love.

It is easier to speak or write about love and nonviolence than to practice it. When we were robbed in Berkeley and I was beaten and mugged in Sacramento, we did not feel very loving toward the assailants. Prayers for them and the willingness to forgive eased our pain, but not seeing them again made the possibility of an actual reconciliation impossible. It helps to look the other in the eye and see a person who is loved by God. We need to see the good as well as bad, the hope as well as hurt, in our neighbor.

When Sorokin was dismayed to find few or no references to love in text books of psychology or sociology, he challenged the academic world with the question of what matters most: rocket science or learning to live at peace on earth? In the 1970s, Leo Buscaglia taught a course on the "Love" at the University of Southern California. He said that "we are probably the only university in the country that does such a class . . . love has really been ignored by the scientists."

Sorokin's challenge has not been met. Our verbal claims to cherish peace are hypocritical lies when compared to where and how we spend our wealth. In America, far more is spent on weapons of mass destruction and other arms than on training for peace, conflict resolution, feeding the hungry, clothing the naked, and providing health care for those suffering from various diseases around the world. In 2008, the U.S. is expected to have spent approximately $950 billion on military costs. This is about 43 percent of our budget not counting Social Security and Medicare. The U.S. spends about one percent of its budget on diplomacy.[63]

Our culture reflects what we learn early in life. From viewing old Westerns to playing modern video games, the message is always the same—"kill the bad guys." It's that simple. "You are what you eat," is a saying that is largely true, and our young people are being fed with the poison of a prurient, hypocritical, and violent culture. Should we really be surprised to read of shootings and rapes, cheating and stealing, vandalism and looting, going on in our schools and neighborhoods?

Parental upbringing is of primary importance in forming the attitudes and actions of our young people. But our educational system also has a large role to play, and it could incorporate some significant classes on the subject of valuing all people. We are not advocating teaching religion in our public schools. Ethics, however, is another matter. We are all moral beings; there are certain "rights" and "wrongs" regarding which we agree. To teach about honesty, respect, and love is not teaching a religion; it is teaching about human dignity, human rights, and human needs. If these are not addressed carefully and thoroughly, we cannot expect to live in a just and peaceful world. Dean Ornish describes his book *Love and Survival* as based on a simple but powerful idea: "Our survival depends on the healing power of love, intimacy and relationships . . . As individuals. As communities. As a country. As a culture. Perhaps even as a species."[64]

Joyce and I would love to see our educational institutions incorporate such topics for studying the real meaning of love as how to—
- understand the different levels of love
- handle conflict
- control anger
- be diplomatic
- hear the heart of someone else
- forgive
- understand other cultures
- respect sexuality
- conduct a peaceful demonstration
- prevent escalation of conflict
- help the poor
- confront injustice
- be a peacemaker
- appreciate all races
- value the environment
- be a good steward of what has been entrusted to us
- love our country
- love our world

These are only a few of many topics which can be studied under the broader topic of "Learning How To Love." When we honestly evaluate what is most important in our world, getting to the moon or getting along with our neighbors on earth, then surely the discipline of learning to love must come first. So why not put action behind our words? We can write new textbooks, train our teachers, and improve our required courses. If we practice playing the piano, surely we should also practice learning to love. Nothing could be more worth the effort.

Cultural exchanges with people of other nations can be of tremendous value. Government support for thousands of such adventures would be money well spent. You do not feel like killing someone with whom you have sung and danced, or those with whom you have engaged in sports or shared a sketching trip.

In 1984, Joyce and I participated in a month-long cultural exchange with artists in the Peoples Republic of China. It was a marvelous experience of sharing ideas, paintings, exhibits, food, laughter, and mutual affirmation. At the end of our time there, our "atheist" guide requested a copy of a Chinese-English Bible we had brought along. (We had each brought two copies and had given away all but one, which Joyce was able to give him.) He also showed us a painting he was working on which showed a cross in the window. "There," he said, "is where we will find the guidance we need to do our best in the days ahead."

We were profoundly moved by his comment. We made many friends while in China and wondered how we could ever think of killing these dear people as would happen in a war. Killing is easier for some when they don't see the faces. They are simply labeled "the enemy." But when you become acquainted, you see these folk as precious partners in the great interconnected human family, the family of God.

Elaine Klaasen, in her comments on "Alternatives to Violence Project Goes to Africa" makes a similar observation about the value of people sharing together in a discussion of important issues. She writes,

> The exceptionally creative thing about an AVP workshop is that a new community is forged during the intense, intimate time that people spend together, laughing, playing, thinking, no matter whether the participants be an old Buddhist farmer, a young Baptist university professor, a middle-aged atheist biker... or a politically radical ex-felon. Or a Hutu or a Tutsi.[65]

Community happens when we affirm one another in a venture that is bigger than our differences.

The Peace Corps was a great idea. Those we know who have participated in this program have shared beautiful stories of blessings received, gratitude expressed, aid rendered, and cooperation between neighbors achieved. Can it and comparable programs not be enlarged to include thousands more?

Why not use our military to do constructive projects like slum cleanup in troubled areas of American cities? On the international scale, why not offer all kinds of humanitarian aid to Asia, Africa, or other lands? Our young men and women have volunteered to serve their country. There are thousands of opportunities to serve our country and other nations without the involvement of killing. We must agree with Jim Wallis, who wrote: "In an era aflame with war, the gospel vocation of peacemaking has never been more important. But peacemaking must now be turned into realistic strategies for practically resolving conflicts in a violent world."[66]

There are many ways to overcome the blight of poverty, and the cruelty of injustice. Peace is not an impossible goal. We have the resources. We need the commitment. Killing the enemy is not the answer. Attempting to overcome evil with good puts us on the right track.

Jesus said, "Love your enemies." He wasn't kidding. With God's help, we can do it.

We have been seeking the best ways to bring peace into this world. The Bible uses one word a lot. It expresses a special concern for the well-being of another. It is the word *love*. As a noun it appears about 150 times, as a verb about 350 times. That may well be our best clue.

Chapter Fifteen

We Share Letters of Yearning for Peace

JESUS WEPT WHEN HE ENTERED JERUSALEM on that festive day when he was hailed as the messianic king. The crowds wanted a king who would kill their enemies. But God's way is the opposite. God's love transforms enemies into beloved children. That is as hard for us to grasp as it was for them. So Jesus broke down into sobs as he saw the city (Jerusalem means "city of peace") and said, "If you, even you, had only recognized on this day the things that make for peace!" (Luke 19:41-42). Most of the world continues to be blind to the "things that make for peace."

However, that blindness no longer includes everyone. There is hope. There are excellent books, numerous organizations, churches, synagogues, mosques, and temples with millions of people who are dedicated to living out the "things that make for peace." Our prayer is that after reading the following letters, more will make the same commitment to strive for justice, peace, and love for all of God's children.

TO OUR LIBERAL CHRISTIAN FRIENDS

You have a rich history of social action and addressing injustice. You have reminded the church that faith without works is dead. Jesus calls us to make a positive difference in our world, and you have heard that call.

Your churches were among the first to challenge slavery and racial segregation. You have championed women's rights and gender equality. You have addressed the exploitation of our environment.

When the issues of war and capital punishment come up, your voice has been less clear. Some of you have rallied with your Quaker, Mennonite, and Brethren neighbors to protest the evils of killing. Some of you have participated in antiwar marches and have used nonviolent approaches to defend the poor and redress injustice. We praise God for these actions, even as we believe more can be done.

Our appeal to you is that together our anti-violence message will ring with increasing clarity until all come to recognize that God wills for his children to live in peace with one another. Do we not pray, "Thy will be done on earth as it is in heaven?" There isn't any killing in heaven!

Violence is not a wholesome answer to our world's problems. The better way, taught by Jesus, is to learn how to "overcome evil with good."

One of your finest prophetic preachers, Harry Emerson Fosdick, gave the church one of its profoundest hymns, "God of Grace and God of Glory." In the third stanza we sing the prayer that God will "Cure your children's warring madness" and "make our broken spirits whole." We pray for all of us to recommit our lives to being vessels of God's love for the entire world. Marcus Borg called the early church the "Peace Party in Palestine." Let us be the "Peace Party" for the world in the twenty-first century.

Peace,
Randy and Joyce Klassen

TO OUR CONSERVATIVE CHRISTIAN FRIENDS

Thank you for your continued high regard for biblical authority. It is truly from the early apostles that we gain our clearest picture of Jesus and his inspired words for us. With you, we rejoice in the promises of grace for God's presence with us now and forever.

With you we have also noted that Jesus had some high expectations of us while we are living here on earth. He calls us to be "salt of the earth, light of the world" (Matt. 5:13-14). Jesus reminds us that to be true children of the heavenly Father we are to show love for all, including those called enemies (Matt. 5:44-45). That's quite a challenge! But Jesus goes on to say that this kind of expansive all-embracing, all-inclusive love is to be the distinguishing feature of his followers.

You affirm a pro-life position that is a valid expression of such love. Therefore you oppose abortion. However, life is certainly as precious after birth as before, so when you follow our Lord's teaching, you can take it farther to all who long for an abundant life, all over the world. Far too many of your neighbors in other countries, as well as here at home, have become victims of various forms of violence. By the power of the Holy Spirit, we all need to spread good news for the poor as Jesus did. That includes food, clothing, medicine, housing, protection, all life's basic needs. We pray for all of our churches truly to become beacons of hope to others by sharing of both spiritual and physical bread.

When we put in first place what Jesus said was first—love for God and love for neighbor—surely that will exclude killing the enemy. Let us be true Bible believers and demonstrate our pro-life position to those called enemies.

The Bible leaves us with this amazing challenge: to overcome evil with good (Rom. 12:21). That's God's way and we are to participate in it. Ministries like World Vision are doing just that, as are many of your missionary endeavors.

Will you join us all in recommitting our lives to being true followers of Jesus, our "Prince of Peace" and be the peacemakers he called blessed?

Peace,
Randy and Joyce Klassen

TO OUR CATHOLIC FRIENDS

You have a long tradition of inspiring saints in your history. While we all have some members who have disappointed us, you have many true saints who have permanently and beautifully enriched the human family in many parts of the world. There was Jerome and Saint Francis, Catherine of Sienna and Teresa of Avila, Patrick of Ireland, and Thomas à Kempis, whose book *The Imitation of Christ* has inspired millions. In the twentieth century we came to love Mother Teresa, and her humanitarian ministries, as well as Dorothy Day, co-founder of the Catholic Worker movement, for her courageous witness against war and injustice.

We are also grateful for your late Pope John Paul II. We applauded his ecumenical spirit, his peacemaking travels among Jews and Muslims, and his bold pro-life position. He called his church to honor the sanctity of life by opposing abortion, euthanasia, and capital punishment. He stated his opposition to the U.S.-led 2003 invasion of Iraq. Your late Cardinal Joseph Bernardin of Chicago challenged all pro-life people to be consistent and oppose all violence and war as passionately as abortion.

The love of God does not allow for injustice in any form—whether exploitation of children, oppression of the poor, degradation of women, or discrimination against those of another color or culture.

We have read of one of your ministries of nonviolence by the Sisters of Providence of Saint Mary of the Woods. These sisters issue a call to change heart and mind in a prayerful effort to transform on behalf of justice and peace the world's systems, structures, and institutions.

Let us work together in the loving and demanding art of peacemaking. As you use your many gifts and opportunities for advancing God's kingdom of justice, peace, love, hope, and joy will be spread to many.

Peace,
Randy and Joyce Klassen

TO OUR ORTHODOX FRIENDS

We know only a little about your rich tradition, but we do understand that it includes a strong affirmation of Jesus

Christ as Lord. Together with you, we seek to honor Christ by following his teachings about justice, love, and peace.

It was an inspiration to read of your Bishop Kiril of Bulgaria, who during the Nazi attempts to kill Jews in that region led nonviolent protests against the Nazis. He said he would lie on the tracks before any train carrying Bulgarian Jews off to German concentration camps. The people rallied behind their bishop, and nearly all Bulgarian Jews were saved from the Holocaust. We pray that this courageous bishop will continue to be an inspiration to many in your Orthodox communities to support nonviolent methods in seeking to establish justice and peace.

In the past, your fellowship, like some others, has been unwilling to work with other Christian denominations. Recently, however, some of your churches have been working in cooperation with churches like the Evangelical Covenant, the Mennonite churches, and others to advance the cause of Christ in evangelism, social action, health concerns, and peacemaking. Thank you for opening your heart to your sisters and brothers in other groups. We can all learn from one another

True orthodoxy includes a commitment to justice and peacemaking. We trust you will continue to join others who, like you, are giving themselves to following faithfully the one the Bible calls "The Prince of Peace."

Peace,
Randy and Joyce Klassen

TO OUR JEWISH FRIENDS

Thank you for the rich heritage you have shared with the world. Belief in one God, redemption from slavery, the Ten Commandments, and the prophetic voices for justice are some of the many blessings you have given to people all over our planet.

After the horrors of the Holocaust, we were grateful that your ancient homeland was opened up for you in 1948, to once again become the nation of Israel. We pray that peace with your neighboring nations may be satisfactorily realized. We pray that with the establishing of justice for all—not an easy achievement in that region—there soon will be peaceful and friendly relations between Jews, Muslims, and all others.

We have been encouraged to read of how gardens have been planted by Jews and Arabs working together along the boarders of Palestine and Israel, demonstrating the way of peace. When either government shows signs of willingness to make concessions, we rejoice in a diplomacy of nonviolence.

Your ancient prophet Micah said it so well that Christians and others have also affirmed his emphasis: "What does the Lord require of you but to do justice, and to love kindness, and to walk humbly with your God?" (Mic. 6:8). We want to join in that walk with you.

Your contemporary prophets like Abraham Herschel, Elie Wiesel, and Victor Frankl, have challenged and enriched the lives of so many. As Thomas Cahill has pointed out in his book *Gifts of the Jews*, your gifts to us all are many and for these we are most grateful.

Wherever you live, America or Israel or elsewhere in the world, we want to affirm your every effort to advance the causes of justice and peace through nonviolent means. As your ancient poet said, "O God, . . . your steadfast love is better than life" (Psalm 63:3).

Shalom,
Randy and Joyce Klassen

TO OUR MUSLIM FRIENDS,

Love and peace to you.

Your history, like ours, has been marred by some tragic events, which have obscured the true meaning of our religions. So when we see your people and ours following the ways of love and justice, we rejoice.

It was that kind of sacrificial generosity that caused our hearts to rejoice as we read about how your brothers and sisters sheltered a number of their Tutsi neighbors during the 1990s genocide in Rwanda. The numerous instances of cordial relations with Jews and Christians bear witness to the true intent of Islam. As the Qu'ran records it, "Surely Allah enjoins the doing of justice and the doing of good [to others]" (16:19).

Beautiful examples of nonviolence are found in Islamic history, ranging from the first thirteen years of the Prophet Mohammed's experience in Mecca to more recent events in Lebanon and Palestine. In India, the Muslim leader Abdul Ghaffar Khan mobilized 100,000 soldiers from the Pashtun tribe who pledged to resist the British injustice without doing any violence, echoing Gandhi's call to nonviolence. He rallied them with the call to use the only weapon no power on earth can withstand, "that weapon is patience and righteousness" (as recorded by Mohammed Abu Nimer in *Fellowship* magazine, Sept.-Oct. 2004).

We wish to join heart and hands in the real "Jihad," a spiritual warfare against injustice, poverty, and violence. We pledge to work with you using only those methods that harmonize with the goals of spreading love, justice, and peace in our needy world, as many of your Sufi members are doing.

Peace,
Randy and Joyce Klassen

TO OUR BUDDHIST FRIENDS

Peace and love to you.

We confess at the outset that we do not know very much about your religion. So when we looked into your scriptures, we were encouraged to find some wonderful statements about nonviolence and compassion.

In the Dhammapada 5 it says, "Hatreds never cease through hatred; through love alone they cease. This is an eternal law." It can hardly be said better. May God give us all the strength to live by this law.

Again in the Dhammapada 223, we are told to "Conquer anger by love. Conquer evil by good. Conquer the stingy by giving. Conquer the liar by truth." So it must be to conquer violence. If we respond with violence to violence we only bring forth more violence. As in the Christian Scriptures, your wisdom is to "overcome evil with good."

Your Buddhist Peace Fellowship, founded in 1978, draws on the compassion of Buddhist traditions and practices and on some of the American civil rights, antiwar movements, and other nonviolent faith based movements for addressing injustices and advancing positive social changes. We praise your efforts of opposing the repression in Tibet, Burma, Sri Lanka, Bangladesh, Vietnam, and elsewhere.

We were impressed by your pacifist teacher of Zen Buddhism, Thich Nhat Hanh, now in his eighties, whose emphasis on compassion and forgiveness is truly redemptive. He points out our need to hear each other and understand that we all suffer. Anger only increases the suffering, whereas compassion born in our hearts can enable us to forgive and bring healing. We wholeheartedly agree.

Our prayers will be with you as you seek to involve more of your constituents in your peace ministry. We want to partner with you and with all groups who are committed to addressing the wrongs of this world with loving nonviolent options.

May your Peace Fellowship grow so that its purposes can be fulfilled and all injustice and violence can be conquered by love. We join with you in making this commitment to use every opportunity to advance the causes of justice and peace.

Peace,
Randy and Joyce Klassen

TO OUR HINDU FRIENDS

We admit to knowing little about your religion. As artists, however, we have often been intrigued by the beauty of the colors, patterns, and designs found in your temples and on your festive clothing. But even more impressive is this statement about beauty: "The ornament (beauty) of virtuous persons is their conduct. One should never harm the wicked or the good or even criminals meriting death. A noble soul will ever exercise compassion even toward those who enjoy injuring others." This we found in your sacred writings, Ramayana, Yuddha Kanda 115. There the maxim is underscored that a good Hindu does not render evil for evil.

No one modeled that better than Mohandas K. Gandhi, who taught and practiced nonviolence, calling it "the greatest force humanity has been endowed with."

Compassion and honesty are a major part of your tradition. Long ago one of your scribes wrote, "Let your conduct be marked by truthfulness in word, deed, and thought."

Wherever the challenge may be, in India, Africa, or here in the United States, the way to peace, as you well know, calls for both integrity and compassion which rules out all violence toward fellow humans.

As we strive to be faithful to our Lord, who calls us to model these same virtues, let us join hearts and hands as co-workers in the healing mission of being peacemakers wherever we find ourselves.

Peace,
Randy and Joyce Klassen

TO OUR AGNOSTIC FRIENDS,

Warm greetings to you, dear questioners. God is indeed a mystery. We have all been baffled by that ultimate Reality some of us call God. We need the questions many of you have raised. You often challenge our belief systems, and that has produced healthy dialogue.

One area in our mutual pondering seems to have brought us together. We share the conviction that love and integrity beat hatred and falsehood any day. We agree that society fares much better when there is a commitment to liberty and justice for all people. We are ready to work together in eradicating poverty, crime, and racial and sexual discrimination.

So for the good of our country and our world, we can, for now, put aside our differences in matters of doctrine and philosophy and give ourselves to that most urgent need in our world—the need for justice, liberty, and peace.

Sociologists or psychologists like Pitimir Sorokin, Ralph K. White, and others have recognized the redemptive powers of altruistic love. Cultivating this love-energy probably is the most urgent need of our day. With that we are in agreement.

So, will you join with your friends of many religions, or of no religion, to become actively involved in nonviolent efforts to challenge injustice, eradicate poverty, and advance the dynamic of sister- and brotherhood in a one-world family?

Thank you for your valued partnership.

Peace,

Randy and Joyce Klassen

Conclusion

WE HAVE WONDERED, if every Christian were an active peacemaker, what a difference would be made worldwide! However, this is obviously not the case. Are many so-called Christians not Christian? Many of us have found the label misleading. When asked about being called a Christian in his book, *Finding God in the Questions*, Timothy Johnson replied, "I personally prefer 'follower of Jesus.'"[67] We also have come to prefer such an identification, and believe that every sincere follower of Jesus will reject the options of violence and instead choose the pathways of justice, mercy, and peace. Love allows for no other options.

Because we have seen love spelled out most clearly in Jesus, we encourage readers, Christians or others, to take another look at the life, teachings, ministry, death, and resurrection of the Prince of Peace.

For further study we recommend the books listed under Notes. We also encourage you to consider joining FOR, Fellowship of Reconciliation, a vital interfaith organization that has promoted justice and peace all over the world since 1914. FOR can be reached at PO Box 271, Nyack, NY 10960. Their website is www.forusa.org and email is rpf@forusa.org. Many peace-related resources are also available from Mennonite Central Committee, www.mcc.org.

We thank you for reading our limited attempt to put into words the passionate commitment of our hearts. We wish you God's love, and joy, and peace.

Notes

1. Walter Wink, *The Powers That Be* (New York: Doubleday, 1998), p. 42.
2. Gavin De Becker, *Fear Less* (London: Little Brown & Co., 2002), p. 17.
3. Leo Tolstoy, *A Confession*, trans. Jane Kentish (London: Penguin Books, 1987), p. 198.
4. Ronald Gottesman, ed., *Violence In America*, vol. 1 (New York: Scribner & Sons, 1999), p. xiv.
5. Wink, p. 55.
6. Robert K. Johnston, *Reel Spirituality: Theology and Film in Dialogue* (Grand Rapids, Mich.: Baker Academic, 2003) p. 47.
7. De Becker, pp. 24-25.
8. Bruce Chilton, *Rabbi Jesus* (Doubleday, New York, 2000), p. 12.
9. Ibid., 60.
10. Thomas Merton, "Blessed Are The Meek," in *Peace Is the Way*, ed. Walter Wink (Maryknoll, N.Y.: Orbis Books, 2000), p. 44.
11. Robert Guelich, *The Sermon On The Mount: A Foundation For Understanding* (Dallas: Word Publishers, 1982), p. 92.
12. Jim Wallis, *God's Politics* (San Francisco: Harper San Francisco, 2005), p.160.
13. Wink, *Powers That Be*, p. 101.
14. Gandhi quoted in Ibid., p. 102.
15. Walter Wink, *Jesus and Noviolence* (Minneapolis: Minn.: Fortress Press, 2003), pp. 24-25.
16. Guelich, p. 227.
17. Ibid., p. 228.
18. Marcus J. Borg, *Jesus: A New Vision* (San Francisco: HarperSan Francisco, 1987), p. 139.
19. Richard B. Hays, *The Moral Vision of the New Testament* (New York: Harper Collins, 1996), p. 322.

20. Ibid., p. 337.
21. Elaine Pagels *Adam, Eve and the Serpent* (New York: Random House, 1988), p. 50.
22. Ibid., p. 52.
23. Sir Ernest Bennet quoted in Pitirim Sorokin, *The Ways and Power of Love*, Gateway ed. (Chicago: Henry Regnery Co., 1967), p. 55
24. Tolstoy, p. 188.
25. Borg, p. 138.
26. Tolstoy, p. 188
27. Ibid., p. 189
28. Wink, p. 129.
29. Martin Luther King Jr., *Strength To Love* (Philadelphia: Fortress Press, 1982), p. 21.
30. Ibid., p. 48.
31. Ibid., p. 49.
32. Ibid., pp. 54-55.
33. Chris Hedges, *War Is a Force That Gives Us Meaning* (New York: Anchor Books, 2003), p. 13.
34. Ibid., p. 21.
35. Farley Mowat, quoted Ibid., p. 28.
36. Erich Maria Remarque, quoted Ibid. p. 87
37. King, p. 51.
38. Frederick Nietzsche, *Beyond Good and Evil*, trans. R. J. Hollingdale (New York: Viking Penguin, 2003), p. 102.
39. Sorokin, p. 70.
40. Jim Wallis, *The Soul of Politics* (Maryknoll, N.Y.: Orbis Books, 1994), p. 190.
41. Wink, *The Powers That Be*, 117.
42. Sorokin, pp. 67-68
43. Wink, *The Powers That Be*, p.117
44. Sorokin, pp. 170-171
45. Gandhi quoted in Sharman Apt Russell, *Hunger: An Unnatural History* (New York: Basic Books, 2005), 85.
46. Mohandas K. Gandhi, "Nonviolence—The Greatest Force," in *Peace Is the Way*, ed. Walter Wink (Maryknoll, N.Y.: Orbis Books, 2000), p. 3.
47. Ronald J. Sider and Richard K. Taylor, "International Aggression and Nonmilitary Defense," *Christian Century*, July 6-13, 1983, pp. 643-647.
48. Hildegard Goss-Mayr, "When Prayer and Revolution Become People Power," in *Peace Is the Way*, ed. Walter Wink, p. 253.
49. Sorokin, p. 48.
50. Ibid., p. 52.

51. Ibid., p. 57.

52. Marian Hostetler, *They Loved Their Enemies* (Herald Press, Scottdale, Pa., 1988), p. 56.

53. Peggy Gish Faw, "Neither Violent Nor Victim," in *What Would You Do?* ed. John Howard Yoder (Herald Press, Scottdale, Pa., 1992), pp. 130-134.

54. Angie O'Gorman, "Defense Through Disarmament," in *What Would You Do?* ed. John Howard Yoder, p. 123.

55. Ibid., p. 127.

56. Cornelia Lehn, *Peace be with You* (Newton, Kan.: Faith and Life Press, 1980), p. 46.

57. Corrie Ten Boom with John and Elizabeth Scherrill, *The Hiding Place* (Minneapolis: World Wide Publications, 1971), p. 233.

58. Philip Yancey *What's So Amazing About Grace?* (Grand Rapids, Mich.: Zondervan, 1997), p. 100.

59. Elsa Tamez, *Bible of the Oppressed* (Maryknoll, N.Y.: Orbis Books, 1982), p. 63.

60. Susan Thistlethwaite, ed., *A Just Peace Church* (Cleveland, Oh.: United Church Press, 1986), p. 35.

61. Sorokin, p. v.

62. Ibid, p. vi.

63. Friends Committee on National Legislation,*Washington Newsletter,* March 2008.

64. Dean Hornish, *Love and Survival* (New York: HarperCollins Publishers, 1998), p. 1.

65. Accessed at www.southsidepride.com/0207/News/alternatives_to_violence.htm.

66. Wallis, *God's Politics*, p. xxi.

67. Timothy Johnson, *Finding God In The Questions* (Downers Grove, Ill.: InterVarsity Press, 2004), p. 135.

The Authors

RANDY AND JOYCE KLASSEN, Walla Walla, Washington, are retired after doing freelance art for six years and then developing a new church in California and reviving another in Arizona. Randy was also pastor of established churches or founder of new ones for over forty years.

Now they are enjoying life in Walla Walla but are not sitting on rocking chairs watching the world go by. Since both are artists, their creative impulses spur them to ongoing creative achievements. Randy also fills pulpits and teaches classes as opportunities come along. Joyce is involved in Community Theater, and that calls for hours of memorization and rehearsing.

Their deeply felt concern for peace in this violent world has led them to give time and effort, hearts and minds to the formation of this book. The call of Jesus to love our enemies has challenged them to ponder its implications and how it can be accomplished, even by ordinary people such as they consider themselves to be. Peacemakers who have taken seriously this call have helped inspire their study.

www.ingramcontent.com/pod-product-compliance
Lightning Source LLC
LaVergne TN
LVHW011355080426
835511LV00005B/299